A SHORT ACCOUNT OF

ORGANS BUILT IN

ENGLAND.

A SHORT ACCOUNT
OF
ORGANS
BUILT IN ENGLAND

from the Reign of *King Charles II*
to the present time

by

SIR JOHN SUTTON

1847

with an introduction by
CANON HILARY DAVIDSON
1979

POSITIF PRESS, OXFORD

Frontispiece: Pencil sketch of Sir John Sutton as a young man. Reproduced by kind permission of the Parochial Church Council of Chollerton.

Printed by Parchment (Oxford) Ltd. and
Bound by Henry Brooks (Bookbinders) Ltd.
in the City of Oxford.

Published by Positif Press, 130 Southfield Road,
Oxford, OX4 1PA

ISBN 0 9503892 9 3

INTRODUCTION

This book was published anonymously; and although Sir John Sutton's authorship of it always seems to have been an open secret, readers will want a more definite reason for attributing the 'Short Account' to him. On page 54 the author describes a Father Smith chamber organ in his possession, and illustrates it at the end of the chapter. This instrument is now (1978) owned by Mr. N. P. Mander, the London organ-builder, and inside is a note in Sir John Sutton's hand and with his signature, stating how he found the organ and bought it. This seems as conclusive a proof as is needed.

Sir John Sutton

John Sutton was born on 18th October 1820, first child of Sir Richard Sutton, Bart., of Norwood Park near Southwell in Nottinghamshire, and his wife Mary Elizabeth, daughter of William F-W. Burton, of Burton Hall, County Carlow in Ireland. Sir Richard, the second baronet, was a great huntsman – his name was a household word among fox-hunters in the first half of the nineteenth century. His enthusiasm for hunting and shooting did not preclude other activities; he played the flute, and was a lover of books. John was the eldest of seven brothers and four sisters, and after a period under a private tutor, and probably with a clergyman training up boys for public schools, he went to Eton College for two years. We do not know whether he was happy there or not, but in 1836 he was placed with the Revd. Christopher Bird, Vicar of Chollerton near Hexham in Northumberland, where he stayed until he was twenty-one years old. Christopher Bird was a great character; he held degrees from both Oxford and Cambridge, specialising in classics and mathematics. He was an advocate of Catholic emancipation, and like many clergy of his day, was keenly and practically interested in the welfare and housing of the poor.

In 1841, John was admitted Fellow-Commoner at Jesus College, Cambridge. Twenty years before, this College had become conspicuous for the growth in the number of its undergraduates, and particularly in the number of its Fellow-Commoners. These, in that rank-conscious age, were recruited from families of substance, and especially the nobility. Monetarily, they were of some advantage to a College as they paid double fees, but a considerable proportion of them never proceeded to a degree, nor probably ever intended to. They were admitted to the Fellows' table in Hall, to the Fellows' Combination Room afterwards, and even (a conclusive sign of social standing) to the College cellar. They often gave a non-reading tone to a College; but there are exceptions to every rule, and John seems to have been one of them. Admittedly, he never proceeded to a degree, but we have it from his own lips that he followed the normal course of studies prescribed at the time – probably specialising in Latin and Greek, in the first of which languages he was unusually proficient. He spent his vacations (and probably most of his spare time in the terms) in collecting the material for this book; and at a time when travel was by no means so simple as it was to become even thirty years later, the amount of information the book contains is remarkable in the number of miles it represents.

On 23rd December 1844, soon after leaving the University, John married Miss Emma Helena Sherlock, daughter of Colonel Francis Sherlock of Southwell; but the new Mrs. Sutton died only a month after her wedding, and John was left to mourn her, and to try to occupy his mind in some way. He does not seem to have shared any of his father's passions for the chase and was, one imagines, very grateful when he was invited back to Cambridge later in 1845. The reason for this was that the Master and Fellows of Jesus College had decided to restore the College chapel, which is part of the medieval priory church of St. Radegunde. The restoration of the chapel proved to be a complicated and even dangerous business, as part of the roof collapsed during the work; and in the end the original architect, Anthony Salvin, was dismissed and A. W. N. Pugin (on John's recommendation) appointed in his place. I believe John Sutton and Pugin had met and become friends some years before; but in any case, they were to be thrown together a good deal now, and one can imagine that John gained a great deal of his knowledge of Gothic architecture and art, and the principles underlying it, from his friend. Augustus Pugin (his life spanned the years 1812-1852) was a genuine medievalist; he had a burning passion for everything Gothic, and went so far as to apply the title 'Christian Architecture' to one particular style, the Early English (as it is called in England) or second pointed. This passion for Gothicism extended to the Church that the Gothic buildings were created to serve and Pugin became a Roman Catholic (though a singularly independent one) in 1835. He contributed the drawings of suggested model organ-cases that are printed at the end of this book − and it is fair to say that his organ-cases look far better when built than they do on paper. Two of them, perhaps the only ones ever made to his designs, were for John Sutton; they were at Jesus College chapel itself, and the family church at West Tofts in Norfolk (since this church was closed in 1941, the organ is now at South Pickenham nearby).

But even a restored college chapel is a dead thing without the worship it is intended to shelter, and well before the work was finished, intoned services (as opposed to the priest's part being merely read, as was the nearly universal custom in England) were begun in the dining hall by the Dean and Chaplain. John Sutton was asked to be organist, and having brought in the little organ mentioned on our first page, took a further part in the revival of the classical Anglican worship of his college by recruiting a choir. We don't know whether there were men in it or not, but the boys came fresh from their homes in the town. John educated them himself, not only in music and singing, but in the normal elementary subjects; and it is recorded that he was so devoted to their well-being that he remained in Cambridge during the greater part of the university vacations to teach them.

Jesus College Chapel, restored and glorious, was re-opened on All Saints' Day, 1st November 1849. John Sutton had provided the organ, the altar, and the great lectern, and paid for the floor tiles and the decoration of the roof. The service was a fully choral Mattins, Litany and Holy Communion. John directed the choir, and the Professor of Music, T. A. Walmisley, played the organ. He also composed a setting of Psalm 5, *"Ponder my words, O Lord"*, for the service. This is for four boys' voices, and shows how proficient the choir was.

The work of furnishing the chapel was continued by the publication, in 1850, of a book of words of the anthems to be sung on Sundays, holy days and their eves. It is a compilation of some size, eighty-eight anthems in all, divided into full anthems and verse anthems; so on occasion men must have joined the boys. Charles Whittingham, who printed this book, printed the anthem-words, but a small number of hymns appear to have been bound in later, printed by a different craftsman, and with many of their tunes by J. B. Dykes. The anthem collection is fairly representative for its time, although one of the most significant omissions is the name of Henry Purcell, certainly one of the greatest of English composers.

It is reasonable at this point to ask who had directed John's taste in music up to the point where he was ready to stand on his own feet as a critic and chooser of what was most worth performing, and most fitting for use in worship. There is not much that can be said about George Skelton, organist of Lincoln Cathedral from 1794, from whom we can conjecture that John had his first music lessons. Much the same, unfortunately, is true of William Henshaw, organist of Durham Cathedral while John was at Chollerton Vicarage. Neither man is mentioned in books like Bumpus's *'History of English Cathedral Music'*, probably because they did not publish any music of their own. John, however, rated Henshaw the foremost Cathedral organist in Britain – probably because of his skill as an accompanist – and was so friendly with him that when the cathedral organ was rebuilt in 1844, he secured two of the discarded stops for inclusion in the Jesus College instrument of 1847-8.

The one person of whose musical influence on John we can be certain was Thomas Attwood Walmisley (1814-56), Professor of Music at Cambridge from 1836 until his death. He had a most distinguished musical ancestry: his godfather and tutor in advanced musical studies was Thomas Attwood, organist of St. Paul's Cathedral, and himself a pupil of Mozart. He it was who first recognised the genius of Mendelssohn in England, and he often invited him to his house in the London suburb of Norwood. Walmisley's predecessor at Cambridge had not even been required to reside at the University: Walmisley himself lived, at least for a time, at Jesus College, where John Sutton had every opportunity to make friends with him. "In knowledge of musical history and general cultivation", says Bumpus, "he was in advance of most English musicians . . . he spoke of J. S. Bach's *Mass in B minor* as the greatest composition in the world, and prophesied that the publication of the cantatas (then in manuscript) would show that his assertion of Bach's supremacy was no paradox. It may confidently be said that the number of English musicians who, in 1840, were acquainted with any music by the great Leipsic cantor, beyond the '*Forty-eight Preludes and Fugues*' might be counted on the fingers: and Walmisley fearlessly preached to Cambridge men the same musical doctrines that Schumann and Mendelssohn enforced in Germany" (*History of English Cathedral Music*). So Bach became one of John Sutton's favourite composers, together with Handel, Mozart and Beethoven; but, true to the spirit of his age, he himself excelled at extemporization, and could reproduce the styles of all four great men at will. In those days it was part of a Cathedral organist's duty and joy to improvise an introduction to the anthems sung daily at Mattins and Evensong; naturally, this could only be done well by imitating the style of the work to be performed. John, whose great joy was to accompany voices, would obviously have worked hard at this branch of musical art.

Somehow the Continent beckoned all the time. John had taken his first trip up the Rhine as far as Switzerland whilst with Christopher Bird at Chollerton, and from 1848 on, he visited Belgium annually. We know that Pugin gave him an introduction to the Belgian architect and glass-painter, Baron Jean de Bethune, and it may have been under his guidance that John began to gather his knowledge of the art treasures of the Low Countries. He was also introduced to Canon Felix Bethune, Baron Jean's brother, and it was before Canon Bethune that he embraced the Roman Catholic faith at Roulers in 1854. From now on he lived principally in Belgium and Germany, visiting England only occasionally, as when he was High Sheriff of Nottinghamshire in 1867. However, he remained on friendly terms with his family, and several of them used to visit him when at length he had homes of his own. There were two — one in the Gouden-Hand-Straat in Bruges, and the second at Kiedrich (or Kiederich as it is sometimes spelt) near Wiesbaden in the Rheingau, Germany. After his conversion, and even after succeeding to the baronetcy in 1855, he had a small household and spent very little of a large income (between £30,000 and £40,000 a year) on himself. Bruges and Kiedrich were the scenes of his greatest benefactions, though very many poor people were helped by him wherever he happened to be. At Bruges, he attached himself to the church of St. Gillis, where there was a choir to be put on its feet, and trained to sing Palestrina's music. The great work in Bruges was the setting-up of the English Seminary — a college to train young men from Belgium, England and Germany for the priesthood, with English sea-ports as the primary places of their future work. A psychologist has suggested that the underlying idea was the importation of the Gothic religion into England; whether this was actually so or not, we shall never know, but certainly some priests, mainly Belgians, were sent to England in due course. However, John never settled any endowment upon this Seminary, so after his death it had to be closed.

A far better fate, happily, befell the other great object of

John's generosity, the choir school at Kiedrich in the Rheingau. This dates from medieval times, which was an immediate 'draw' for him; and in addition, there was a partly medieval organ in the parish church, itself a glorious, lofty, early-Gothic building. And the music sung by the choir had been up until 1817 (and is now since 1865) the medieval Kurmainzer plainsong. This is the variant sung until the seventeenth century in all the churches of the ancient Archbishopric of Mainz, standing in the same sort of relationship to the Vatican texts as the English Sarum variant. The village of Kiedrich has steep streets and half-timbered houses — altogether, just the sort of place an out-and-out medievalist must have dreamed of, and in the 1860's, nearly every part of it in dire need of restoration. Here John bought another house, which he had rebuilt, and in due course the church was restored, the organ made into what John felt it must have looked like when it was first built, and the choir had new statutes, new service-books, English surplices and an endowment. Although most of the money was lost in 1903, and in the inflationary years after 1918, the choir still exists and flourishes, and on 27th December 1965 celebrated the centenary of their re-founding as a corporate body. There has always been a Chorregent or choirmaster, and until recently by statute in priest's orders; and several of these have raised the standard of the music performed, until now the choir is the equal of those in many cathedrals.

Other Rhineland churches benefited from John's generosity; for instance Eltville, Frauenstein and possibly Oberwalluf, all had the benefit of his advice and money towards the restoration of their organs or the provision of new ones. We know, too, that he had the cathedral organ at Freiburg-im-Breisgau rebuilt, although this gift was not as complete an instrument as he had hoped because of his early death. Other examples of his munificence may come to light as time goes on, but he was such a modest and self-effacing man that one imagines he was happiest when nobody but himself knew who had given the money in any of the cases concerned. So it is that we know of no Roman Catholic church in England that received a gift from him – but surely there must have been some. For instance, John's youngest sister, Frances, married the eldest son of Ambrose March Phillipps de Lisle, one of the great figures of the Roman Catholic revival in England, and like John himself, a Gothicist and friend of Pugin. After her early death Frederick Heathcote Sutton, John's youngest brother, designed a memorial window in the private chapel at Grace Dieu in Leicestershire, but there is no mention of John taking any part in this work, though his letters speak eloquently of his sorrow. We do know of one other church in Belgium where Sutton generosity helped out; this is at Vijvekapelle in West-Vlaanderen, where an ancient Dutch organ's front was copied and a one-manual organ built behind it.

There are of course tales about the English baronet still told in Kiedrich: the bag of sovereigns he kept on his desk, from which any poor person who called would receive a golden pound; the spiral staircase, supposedly built to prevent ladies in crinolines getting upstairs; the lord-of-the-manor way he shifted furniture in the church at dead of night so that the restoration would go the way he wanted – and no doubt these tales have lost no fat in the telling. Strangely for one so concerned with details, very much of his work was done through a third party: in Germany, this was one Mgr. Schneider, who was on the staff of the Episcopal Seminary in Mainz and who acted as the go-between with all sorts of people, from the Canons of the Cathedral to the greengrocer (several lists of provisions exist!) and it seems likely that Mgr. Boone of Bruges, originally assistant priest at St. Gillis, acted in a similar way for the Belgian schemes. John was always a gentle, retiring figure; perhaps the Rhinelanders, with their hearty, wine-flavoured ways, overawed him a little – and certainly every generous man finds himself surrounded by people with excellent schemes for him to use his money on. But if he seldom appeared in public in Kiedrich, except in church, he travelled about a good deal – Cologne, Freiburg, Mainz and Frankfurt often appear at the head of his letters, as well as Bruges and Kiedrich. The last few letters we have are charming – full of concern for his manservant, who had contracted tuberculosis and whom John had taken to Aixle-Bains in France to recover his health. This seems to have been accomplished; but when they returned to Bruges, John himself contracted rheumatic fever, and died in June 1873. He was buried in Sint-Kruis cemetary. His tomb-stone was designed by Bethune, and the inscription reads:

Pray for the soul of Sir John Sutton, Bart.,
of Norwood, Notts., England: who, full of good works,
died on June 5th 1873, aged 53.
On whose soul and all Xtian souls may God have mercy.
Amen.

The last part – a normal enough epitaph for a Roman Catholic in any age – copies dozens of such sentences on the tombs of medieval knights and noblemen throughout England. In the Gothic language, Norman-French, they read, ''*Dieu sa alme eyt merci.*'' This was the final Gothicism of a life-long Gothicist.

A Short Account of Organs

What did John Sutton, organist and fellow-commoner of Jesus College in the University of Cambridge, set out to do in '*A Short Account of Organs?*' If we ignore the first section of the book, the Preface and Introduction, it seems that he intended to give a list of the organs thought to have been built by the principal English organ-builders of 1660-1840, with a description of the tonal characteristics of each man's work, the stops he usually included in his instruments, and what was known of the man himself. To a great extent, he succeeds in this: and the lists themselves are an impressive piece of evidence on the distances he must have travelled to see various organs, and the care with which he listened to them when found.

Quite recently, several organ note-books from the late eighteenth and early nineteenth centuries have come to light and work on them has revealed a good many similarities, not only in the actual lists of organ specifications, but also in the comments on the various instruments by the compilers of the notes. However, most recent work has ignored John Sutton's lists in this book, mainly because they are merely lists of churches or chapels where a given organ-builder constructed organs, without a table of the manuals and stops of every instrument. The one writer to mention them, Dr. Boeringer of Susquehanna University, does so only to say that he believes it unlikely that John Sutton could have visited all the organs he cites by 1847, and thinks he must have had access to one of the earlier collections, or to a common source. This is not borne out by close analysis of the Sutton lists and the text of this book. We have to remember that the family owned several houses, and that John himself lived in Northumberland for some years as well as in Cambridge, and was happiest when doing things on his own. The whole of the London organs could have been visited from the 'town house', Cambridge House, Piccadilly (cf. page 61). We know that John went to Oxford because he bought a Father Smith organ from the Warden and Fellows of New College, at which time the family seat in Norfolk was at Lynford Hall near Mundford, and King's Lynn was the nearest large town. Add to this the claim on page 62, that these are the organs by Harris with which the writer is acquainted, and the districts which a visitor to any centre might well explore, and only the cathedrals such as Bristol, Winchester and Salisbury are left. A cathedral always attracts an ecclesiologist and organlover, and there was no shortage of money for long trips by coach, though by 1845 the railways were beginning to spread over the country. It seems right to believe that Sutton did visit the great majority of the organs in his lists, if not all of them, and the lists themselves, the first of their kind published in England, were used by, for instance, Hopkins and Rimbault (whose massive book, '*The Organ: its History and Construction*' was first published in 1855) as the foundation for their own lists.

John Sutton's description of the tone of the organs of this first classical period of organ-building (1665-1720) is of immense value because he heard them almost exactly as they were built. Certainly, extra departments could have been added, or Echos converted into Swells; but usually the pipe-work of the Great and Choir (or better, Chair) soundboards remained reasonably original when he visited them. Often they must have been full of dirt, and the action getting very irregular and perhaps in sore need of attention. However, from 1660 to 1800 English organ-playing and registration followed very definite, almost crystallized, rules and methods: unlike the history of the instrument since about 1880, people's tastes in tone and chorus-building did not alter every thirty years. While tone certainly changed – see what John Sutton said about Father Smith and Samuel Green – the basic design of the organ chorus hardly altered at all, and the names of the knobs controlling the stops of the Great departments looked very similar from organ to organ. Unless, then, some very individualistic organist had had drastic alterations made to the instrument he played, John often found the authentic work and sound of Smith, Harris and Snetzler. This strong, sharp sound he liked, and indeed preferred to what he often found in the work of his own time.

He wrote the '*Short Account*', then, more than partly to emphasize this preference and because by the 1840's many of the most typical old organs were facing a re-building or perhaps even replacement. He was trying to halt the tide of destruction he feared would overwhelm them. We can see this from the first two pages of his own introduction. In most young men such an attachment to the work of the past would seem strange, for youth is generally on the side of contemporary movements, and John Sutton was only 27 when this book was published. But the whole atmosphere inspired by Pugin looked towards the past: Pugin himself, of course, looked right back to the Middle Ages for his perfect period, but one can't do that with organs, apart from their cases, so John Sutton looked to the time when the first classical period of English organ-building began, and this he took as his golden age. Even so, he lived in an exciting time for organ-lovers, because a second classical period was beginning under the leadership of, amongst others, H. J. Gauntlett and William Hill; and he acknowledges this fact in the foot-note on pages 83 and 84. Musical minds all over the country were struggling with the problem of how to complete the tonal scheme of the British organ, so that the works of J. S.

Bach and the other classical composers could be performed as their creators intended. Among these minds was that of T. A. Walmisley, Professor of Music at Cambridge throughout the whole of Sutton's time there, and himself organist of four college chapels. In 1836 he arranged for Gray to make some very significant alterations and additions to the organ at Trinity College (which operation is mentioned on page 37): they included carrying down the compass of nine of the fourteen stops of the Great manual to CCC 16ft., and the provision of two Great to Pedal couplers – one connecting the lowest pedal key with the lowest manual one, and the other with its octave; a more unusual feature still was a Choir to Pedal coupler in superoctave (middle C to the bottom note of the pedal-board), so that solos could be played on the pedals. The pedal-board itself controlled a Sub Bourdon 32ft. only, but such reinforcement of the bass was possible that one can well understand John Sutton complaining about those who 'keep up a perpetual thundering with the pedals' (page 3).

At any period of development and experiment, certain people go too far in certain directions: but even in this Trinity College scheme, there was little to complain about if the resources were used artistically. Perhaps they were, and perhaps they were not; but all over the country at this period, pedals and pedal pipes were being added to old organs. Again, they could have been used artistically; however, there are plenty of organists in our own day who seem to have a compulsion to use pedals, with the 16ft. stops drawn, whenever possible. When they were a new development, and in a sense fashionable, the temptation to polish the bottom octave must have been even stronger than at any subsequent period in the English organ's history.

What John Sutton objected to most strongly was the use of large and heavily voiced organs in the accompaniment of the 'choral service'. What was, and is, this choral service in English cathedrals and collegiate churches? (The following section should be read in conjunction with the English Prayer Book of 1662).

The Cathedral musical establishment consisted of a number of boys, generally between ten and twenty, some men, usually two each to sing the alto, tenor and bass parts, and of course an organist; sometimes there was a choirmaster as well. Two daily services were sung – Morning Prayer and Evening Prayer, or in the old English words, Mattins and Evensong. The actual offices can be set out thus:

Mattins	*Evensong*	
Scripture Sentence	Scripture Sentence	)
Exhortation	Exhortation	)
General Confession	General Confession	) said
Absolution	Absolution	)
Lord's Prayer	Lord's Prayer	)
Versicles and Responses		)
Venite, exultemus Domino (Psalm 95)	Versicles and Responses Psalms	) sung
Psalms		)
Old Testament Lesson	Old Testament Lesson	
Te Deum laudamus (or very rarely, Benedicite omnia opera)	Magnificat, or Cantate Domino (Psalm 98)	) sung
New Testament Lesson	New Testament Lesson	
Benedictus Dominus Deus Israel or Jubilate Deo (Psalm 100)	Nunc Dimittis or Deus Misereatur (Psalm 67)	) sung
Apostles' Creed	Apostles' Creed	(monotoned)
Lord, have mercy upon us	Lord, have mercy upon us	)
Christ, have mercy upon us	Christ, have mercy upon us	) sung
Lord, have mercy upon us	Lord, have mercy upon us	)
Lord's Prayer	Lord's Prayer	(monotoned or sung)
Versicles and Responses	Versicles and Responses	) sung
Collects – one or more of the day, two invariable.	Collects – one or more of the day, two invariable.	
The Anthem	The Anthem	) sung

The five prayers – for the Sovereign, the Royal Family, the Church, the 'Prayer of St. Chrysostom', and the Grace.

To clarify a little further: the Psalms (divided in English use into sixty sections, those for the thirty-first day of the month being those for the thirtieth day repeated) are sung to the Anglican development of the Gregorian chants – as the Venite in Mattins often is too. The other canticles are sung as 'settings', that is, original compositions of more or less elaboration, dating from the sixteenth century to the present day. The versicles and responses also have their settings. The really individual touch is the Anthem or Motet: this can range from an unaccompanied carol in the Christmas season, to a piece of vocal music lasting a quarter of an hour or more by one of the great composers, with organ and orchestral accompaniment. In John Sutton's time it was the custom for the organist to improvise an introduction to the anthem; and we have contemporary accounts of the skill of men such as Walmisley in this art, which no doubt John shared. There would sometimes be an organ piece at the end of the service, though again it might well be an improvisation; there was almost never any organ music before the service. It is worth noting that at All Saints', Margaret Street, London, a church built and furnished twenty years later than this book, after the principles of the Oxford/ Camden Movement, there was no organ music before or after services except on great festivals, though the vocal music was in the cathedral tradition.

In addition to Mattins and Evensong, the Litany would be sung on Sundays, Wednesdays and Fridays, and on Sundays the first half of the Holy Communion, musically comprising the Responses to the Commandments (sometimes called the Kyries) and the Nicene Creed. Composers up to about 1870 did not often write the Gloria in Excelsis because everyone exept those who wished to make their Communions usually left the church after the Prayer for the Whole State of Christ's Church; if there were no communicants, the celebrant and his assistants would leave as well, because the rubrics forbade a Celebration without 'three, or two at the least' to communicate with him. However, it was the custom in some cathedrals and larger churches to use the musical setting of the Sanctus ('Holy, holy, holy, Lord God of Hosts') as an introduction to the Communion Service, as is shown in some early nineteenth-century books, where it states 'To be sung while the priest goes from the desk to the altar'.

It will be seen that the music of an English cathedral or collegiate church was entirely the concern of the professional choir; the congregation was not expected to sing at all, as indeed is still the case today unless hymns are sung. If John Sutton was concerned to preserve the ancient organs that were used to accompany such choirs during the seventeenth and eighteenth centuries, what did he advise when an organ-less church wanted to obtain one? Luckily, the organ at Jesus College chapel in Cambridge, designed tonally by him and with a case by Augustus Pugin, survives; and although it has undergone various alterations during its life, it is in very nearly its original state.

Great Organ CC-c''' 49 notes		*Choir Organ*	
Open Diapason	8	Open Diapason (wood)	8
Stopt Diapason	8	Stopt Diapason	8
Principal	4	Principal	4
Stopt Flute	4	Open Flute	4
Twelfth	$2^2/3$		
Fifteenth	2	One octave of pedals,	
Tierce	$1^3/5$	coupled to Choir keys.	
Sesquialtra ($1^1/3$)	II	Great/Pedal coupler.	
		Built by J. C. Bishop,	
		1847-9.	

Such an instrument, voiced throughout on light pressure, would be perfectly adequate for the accompaniment of the services, and the voices, I have described.

John Sutton dismisses the English parish church tradition of his day pretty shortly. In town churches, an anthem might be sung during a Sunday service; more usually, in town and country alike, metrical arrangements of one or two Psalms were all that a music-lover could expect, perhaps one or two to each service. Psalms, canticles and responses were all said antiphonally by priest and clerk, sometimes the congregation would join in with the clerk, and sometimes they remained silent. There were, however, stirrings in the direction of a more worthy musical offering in many places, by 1847: Dr. Rainbow has chronicled the beginnings of the plainsong movement in his book '*The Choral Revival in the Anglican Church 1839-1872*' (Barrie & Jenkins, 1970), and here and there over the whole country there were places where choral and congregational music was taken seriously. Some parishes published their own books of hymns and metrical psalms, but as yet there was no firm tradition to lay over against that of the cathedrals. Only a small organ was needed for what music there was – indeed, most country churches made do with a collection of orchestral instruments. We know that John Sutton designed the organ at South Pickenham church in Norfolk, which was built originally for West Tofts, the family church of the Suttons. The Great department has exactly the specification set out on page 107 of this book, and the effect is very fine. On such an organ, a solo piece termed 'the middle voluntary' was often introduced after the first lesson at Mattins or Evensong, rather than before or after the service (page 8), as well as the accompaniment to the metrical psalms. Obviously, customs varied from place to place, as they did from cathedral to cathedral, but except in the great town churches, music had but little place in the worship of the English people before about 1860.

In the final chapter, John considers the outward appearance of the organs whose tone he has been describing, and of those he hoped would be built or re-cased as a result of the gothic movement, then gathering power. It is not known if any cases were actually made after the models provided here by Pugin, but though these particular examples are not always attractive as we have them on paper, the two actual organ-cases that we know were designed by him are beautiful indeed: Jesus College Chapel in Cambridge, and South Pickenham church in Norfolk. Both possess most charming pieces of furniture, and a 'school' of case-designers seems to have grown up, amongst whom John Sutton's youngest brother, Frederick Heathcote, was one of the most successful. He, in point of fact, departed from the gothic style as often as he followed it – a fine design for the organ that stood for a time in the south transept of St. Paul's Cathedral exists, in complete harmony with Wren's glorious seventeenth-century building. Up and down the country, there are a number of most pleasing organ-cases in the Pugin-Sutton tradition, of original and unforced design (and these do not include the many very acceptable 'organ-builders' gothic' examples). Whether the architects and other creators of these cases had read this book or not, it is certain that the Sutton circle began a movement in organ-case design for which English people should be permanently grateful.

It is true to say that '*A Short Account of Organs*' fell on deaf ears: there is now no chorus of stops made by Father Smith remaining. There are chamber organs, and odd couples of stops here and there, but nothing from which we can hear what a cathedral or major church organ by Smith sounded like. Similarly, hardly any Harris choruses remain to us, and the same tale, with small variations, can be told about all the organ-builders whose work John Sutton described.

Hill, Gray, Bishop and Bevington, the principal organ-builders of the eighteen-forties, were soon to be joined by Willis, Lewis, Walker, Harrison and many others; and if new organs were ordered from them, as became the fashion in the second half of the nineteenth century, it was not common practice to restore the old organ and re-sell it – particularly as 'the old brilliant tone' was getting less and less popular in the face of organs with vastly increased power, and the ability to imitate many orchestral instruments. So we are dependent upon John Sutton for the knowledge we have about many English organs that are no more; and this re-printing of his book will give musical historians the chance to read for themselves the words that have been quoted so often since he wrote them.

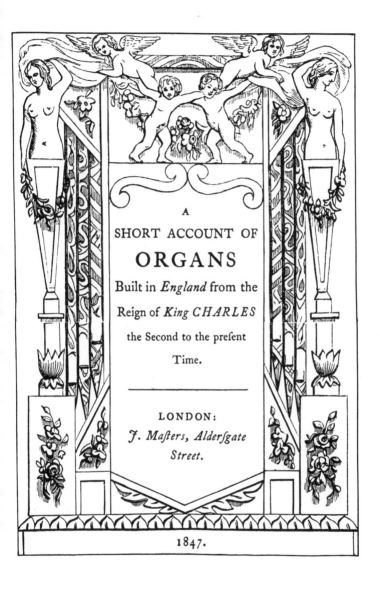

A

SHORT ACCOUNT OF

ORGANS

Built in *England* from the

Reign of *King CHARLES*

the Second to the present

Time.

LONDON:

J. Masters, Aldersgate

Street.

1847.

PREFACE.

IT will be feen that the following pages take no notice of the conftruction of any Organs in this country before the works of the celebrated Father Smith. But though the period of this famous builder and his contemporaries is fo much in advance of any thing that preceded it, as to juftify this commencement, yet it may be worth while, by way of preface, to fay a few words about one or two builders who did practife in this country at the times of the Reſtoration, and before the appearance of Smith.

Loofemore, who was an Exeter man, conſtructed the Organ in the Cathedral of that city, very ſhortly after 1660. This inſtrument is peculiarly remarkable as exhibiting an early inſtance of the adoption of the Double Diapaſon in this country, though it does not appear to have been altogether ſuccefsful if we may judge from the following remarks of the Hon. Roger North.* " His lordſhip, agreeably to his great maſterſhip of muſick, took great notice of the Organ in the Cathedral Church of Exeter, where the two ſide columns that carry the tower, are lined with organ pipes, and are as columns themſelves. His lordſhip deſired the

---

* Life of the Lord Keeper Guilford, by the Hon. Roger North. Vol. I. page 246.

dimenſions of the great double Diapaſon; and the account, as returned,
is thus :

Speaking part, long . . .	20 feet	6 inc.
Noſe	4	o
Circumference	3	11
Diameter	1	3
Content of the ſpeaking part	3 hogs.	8 gall.
Weight	360 lbs.	

This is heard plainer at a diſtance
than when near, as alſo louder ; and,
behind that, and the other large
Doubles, are placed large wooden
pipes to help them into their ſound,
which otherwiſe would come on
very ſlow, or perhaps not at all. One,
being near enough, may by the touch
of the hand, diſcern when it ſpeaks,
and when not. How it is tuned,
whether by meaſure or the beats, we
were not informed ; and, bating their
account of it, which was curious and
diverting enough, I could not be ſo

happy to perceive that in the mufick, they fignified any thing at all, but thought them made more for oftentation than ufe : for there are terms in found which will not be exceeded, for when the vibratory pulfes are fo flow as may be diftinguifhed, found vanifheth; which is nearly the cafe with this great pipe." The " great Pipes" alluded to in this quotation, after ftanding in filent fhow for more than a century and a half, have now at length been made to fpeak by the affiftance of modern bellows, &c. the effect of which exploit is to make the hearer fincerely wifh that the trouble had been fpared, and that the pipes had been left in their original harmleffnefs. Some of Loofemore's work exifts in the inftrument, notwithftanding the alterations of modern days; and there is another fmaller inftrument in the Chorifters'

Singing-School, from the hands of the fame builder, though it is preferved more for curiofity than ufe.*

The following fpecimen of an agreement between Loofemore and a cuftomer may perhaps amufe the reader:

February the 1ᵗʰ 1665.
Then made a bargaine wᵗʰ Sʳ Gᵉᵒ Trevilyan for an Organ wᵗʰ thefe ftops in it as followe.

one diapafon
one flute
one Recorde   } thefe in wood
one fifteenth

---

* Its ftops, which are all of wood, are as follows:

Stop Diapafon.   Twelfth.
Open Diapafon.   Fifteenth.
Principal.   Flute.

Its compafs is C C (fhort octave) to C in alt.

one Principall
one flagilett   } thefe in mettle
one Trumpett
one fhaking ftopp.

And for this organ I am to have one hundred pound 20*l* whereof at the 25th day of march next & fourefcore refidue thereof when the work is finifhed.

JOHN LOOSEMORE.

on the left	on y[e] right
1 Record[r]	Principall
2 flute	Flagilett
3 Diapafon	Ffifteenth
5 Trumpet	

A more celebrated man than Loofemore, and indeed than any other of his time, was Ralph Dallans, but the remains of his handiwork are unfortunately very fcanty. Amongft thofe known we may reckon the Organ of the parifh Church of Rugby,

Northamptonſhire; and Anthony a'
Wood ſays, that he alſo built the
inſtrument for the Muſick School at
Oxford, and that it contained four
ſtops. Now at the preſent time there
exiſts ſtill in the ſchool a ſmall
Organ, evidently of this date; it
may poſſibly be the identical inſtrument. It now contains ſix ſtops,
and has a modern ſet of keys; but
an inſcription upon it informs us that
it was repaired by Samuel Green in
1770.

Two other reſpectable builders
were, Preſton of York, and Thamar
of Peterborough, but the writer cannot refer to any inſtrument remaining of their conſtruction.

The catalogue of Organs that eſcaped the fury of the Parliamentary
troops is very ſhort. Here follow
ſome of the chief inſtances:

St. Mary Magdalen Coll. Oxford.

For this inftrument it is related that Cromwell had really fome affection, from old recollection of its charming tones; a circumftance which will appear lefs improbable if we remember that Judge Jefferies was alfo an Organ fancier, and was actually the umpire between Schmidt and Harris in the conteft for the honour of fupplying the Temple Church. And in fact, the Ufurper did remove the Organ to Hampton Court, where it was played upon by a private Organift for his fpecial amufement. The ftolen property was reftored by the Stuarts, and remained in the College Chapel till the earlier part of the laft century, when it gave place to another inftrument, and is now in the Abbey Church of Tewkfbury.

York Cathedral. The following account of this inftrument is taken from Mr. Stimpſon's deſcription of the Town Organ of Birmingham. It was built by an artiſt named Dallom, and the agreement and other documents relative to it, are ſtill preſerved in the archives of the chapter houſe at York. The ſum required for building the Organ, was furniſhed by Charles the Firſt, who granted the "dean and reſidentiaryes" the ſum of one thouſand pounds, (being a fine which had been "impoſed and ſett" upon one Edward Paler, of Thoralby, in the county of York,) for the purpoſe of "repaireing the ruines of the cathedral church, for ſetting up a *newe organ*, for furniſhing and adorning the altar, and enabling them to maintayne a library keeper." On the receipt of this ſum, Dr. John Scott, dean of the cathedral, with the other principal officers of the church, entered into an agreement with Robert Dallom, " cittizen and blackſmith" of London, " touchinge the makinge of a great organ, for the ſaid church." In the body of the agreement are mentioned " the names and number of the ſtoppes or ſetts of pipes for the ſaid great organ, all of which are to be newe made; every ſtopp containeinge fiftie-one pipes; the ſaid great organ containeinge eight ſtoppes:—

Imprimis. Two Open Diapaſons of
    tynn, to ſtand in ſight, many of them
    to be chafed * . . . . lxxx. *li.*
Imprimis. One Diapaſon ſtopp of wood   x. *li.*
Imprimis. Two Principals of tynn . xxiiij. *li.*
Item. One Twelft of the Diapaſon . viij. *li.*
Item. One ſmall Principal of tynn . vj. *li.*
Item. One Recorder Uniſon to the ſaid
    ſmall Principal . . . . . . vi. *li.*

* This chaſing of the pipes is alſo found at Tewkeſbury.

Item. One Two-and-Twentieth . .   v. *li.*

Item. The great Sound-board, with conveyances,wind-chefts,carrayges, and conduits of lead . . . . .   xl. *li.*

Item. The Roller-board, carrayges and keyes . . . .   xx. *li.*

The names and number of ftoppes of pipes for the choire organ, every ftopp containeinge fiftie-one pipes, the faid choire organ containeinge five ftoppes.

Imprimis. One Diapafon of wood .   x. *li.*

Item. One Principal of tynn, to ftand in fight, many of them to be chafed   xii. *li.*

Item. One Flute of Wood . . . .   viij. *li.*

Item. One fmall Principal of tynn .   v. *li.*

Item. One Recorder of tynn, Unifon to the voice . . . .   viij. *li.*

Item. The Sound-board, Wind-cheft, Drawing Stops, conveyances and conduits . . . .   xxx. *li.*

Item. The Rowler-board, carrayges, and keyes . . . .   x. *li.*

Item. The three Bellows, with Wind-trunckes, and Iron Workes, and other things thereto . . . . .   x. *li.*

This inftrument alfo efcaped the rebels, and is probably the identical fabric thus defcribed by Mafter John Mace, lay clerk of Trinity College, Cambridge, who knew the inftrument, being fhut up in the city of York during the fiege in 1644.*
" Now here you muft take notice that they had then a *Cuftom in that Church* (which I hear not of in any other *Cathedral*, which was) that always before the *Sermon*, the *whole congregation fang a Pfalm*, together with the *Quire and the Organ;* And you muft alfo know, that there was then a moft *Excellent-large-plump-lufty - full - fpeaking - Organ*, which coft (as I am credibly informed) a *Thoufand Pounds*. This *Organ*, I fay, (when the *Pfalm* was fet before

---

* Mace's Mufick's Monument.   Page 18.
Printed 1676.

the *Sermon*) being let out, into all its *Fulnefs of Stops*, together with the *Quire* began the *Pfalm*. But when *That vaft-concording-Unity* of the whole *congregational - Chorus*, came (as I may fay) *Thundering in*, even fo, as it made the very *Ground fhake* under us; *(Oh the unutterable ravifhing Soul's delight !)* In which I was fo *tranfported*, and *wrapt* up into *High contemplations*, that there was no room left in my *whole man*, viz. *Body*, *Soul* and *Spirit*, for any thing below *Divine* and *Heavenly Raptures*. This Organ perifhed in the unfortunate fire of York Minfter in 1829." Mafter Mace feems to have exercifed himfelf a little in Organ building as an amateur, according to the following paffage, which is a defcription of a Chamber Organ made by himfelf at his houfe in Cambridge, of which he gave a plate in

Mufick Monument.* "Now as to the *Defcription* of *This Table Organ*, I cannot more conveniently do It, than firft, in giving you *a View* of It, by *this figure* here *Drawn*, and then by telling you all the *Dimenfions*, and the whole order of It, (I mean my *fecond*, which is the *Largeft*, and the *Beft*) And take as Here followeth *Two* of fuch *Organs* only (I believe) are but as yet in *Being*, in the *World;* They being of my own *Contrivance;* and which I cauf'd to be made In my *own Houfe*, and for my *own Ufe*, as to the maintaining of *Publick Conforts &c.*

It is in Its *Bulk, and Height* of a very *Convenient, Handfom,* and *Compleat Table-Scize ;* (which may *Become* and *Adorn a Noble-Mans Dining Room*) All of the *Beft* fort of *Wainfcot.*

---

* Mufick Monument, p. 242.

The *Length* of the *leaf* 7 *foot* and 5 *Inches* The *Breadth* 4 *Foot*, and 3 *Inches*.

The *Heighth* 3 Foot, *Inch*, and *Better*. *Beneath* the *Leaf*, quite Round, is *Handſom Carv'd*, and *Cut-Work*, about 10 *Inches Deep*, to let out the *Sound:* And *Beneath* the *Cut-Work*, *Broad Pannels*, ſo contriv'd, that they may be taken down at any time, for the *Amending* ſuch *Faults* as may happen; with 2 *Shelv'd Cubbords* at the *End* behind, to *lock* up your *Muſick Books*, *&c.* The *Leaf* is to be taken in 2 Pieces at any time for conveniency of *Tuning*, or the like, *Neatly Joyn'd* in the *Midſt*.

The *Keys*, at the upper End, being of *Ebony*, and *Ivory*, all cover'd with a *Slipping Clampe*, (anſwerable to the other End of the *Table*) which is to take off at any time, when the *Organ* is to be uſ'd, and again put on, and *Lock'd* up; fo that none can know it is an *Organ* by fight, but a *Compleat New-Fafhion'd Table.*

The Leaf has in It 8 *Defks*, Cut quite through very *neatly* (anfwerable to that *Up-ftanding One*, in the *Figure.*) with *fprings* under the *Edge* of the *Leaf*, fo Contriv'd, that they may *Open*, and *Shut* at *Pleafure;* which (when *fhut down*) *Joyn Clofely* with the *Table-Leaf;* But (upon occafion) may be *Opened*, and fet up, (with a *Spring*) in the manner of a *Defk*, as your *Books* may be fet againft Them.

Now the *Intent* of *Thofe Defks*, is of far more *Excellent ufe*, than for meer *Defks;* For without *Thofe Openings*, your *Organ* would be but of very *flender ufe*, as to *Confort*, by Reafon of the *Clofenefs* of the *Leaf;* But by the *Help* of *Them*, each *Defk* opened, is as the putting in of ano-

ther *Quickning*, or *Enlivning Stop ;*
so than when all the 8 *Desks* stand
open, the Table is like a *Little
Church Organ*, so *Sprightfully Lusty*,
and *Strong*, that it is too *Loud* for
any *Ordinary Private use ;* But you
may *Moderate That*, by opening only
so many of Those Desks, as you see
fit for your Present use.

There are in *This Table Six Stops*
The first is an *Open Diapason ;* The
Second a *Principal ;* The *Third* a Fifteenth ; The *Fourth* a *Twelfth ;* The
Fifth a *Two and* Twentieth ; And
the *Sixth* a Regal.   There is like-
wise (for a *Pleasure*, and *Light Content*) a Hooboy Stop, which comes
in at any Time, with the *Foot ;*
which *Stop*, (together with the *Regal*) makes the *Voice Humane.*

The *Bellow* is laid next the Ground,
and is made very *Large*, and driven
either by the *Foot* of the Player, or

by a *Cord* at the far end."

St. John's College, Cambridge. This Organ was likewife amongft the fortunate inftruments. The foldiers contenting themfelves with breaking the eaft window of the Chapel. It remained till 1840. The Choir Organ of this inftrument, the writer conjectures to have been of fomewhat later date from the form of the cafe which ftill remains.

King's Coll. Cambridge. Though the Parliamentary Commiffioners did in purfuance of their inftructions order this Organ to be taken down, yet this edict did not extend to the outer Cafe of Henry the Eighth's time, which ftill remains. The pipes were removed and fold, and were fupplied in the reign of William and Mary, probably by Father Smith; at leaft fo tradition feems to imply.

The Organ of Worcefter Cathedral, lately removed, is alſo ſuppoſed to have eſcaped even the extraordinary occaſions of miſchief to which that city was ſubjected.

One obſervation ſhould be made in concluſion. The writer, as it will be ſeen, has occaſionally ſpoken in terms of ſome cenſure of inſtruments, and their builders. He wiſhes it particularly to be underſtood, that in ſo expreſſing himſelf he has conſidered them eccleſiaſtically and not profeſſionally, and that it is ſolely with reference to their ſervice in Churches that he has given an opinion. In any other light he would be ſorry to paſs any judgment upon perſons of more experience than himſelf, or to criticiſe the works of their hands.

CONTENTS.

Contents.

A Short Account of the Organs built in

England, &c.

INTRODUCTION.

THe great deſtruction of the fine old Organs of this country, which has been going on for the laſt ſixty years, and is ſtill going on, has tempted the author of this little book to write a few pages in their defence, with the hope that they may have ſome effect in preventing their wanton deſtruction in future. The general excuſe for removing them from our Churches (though their enemies even acknowledge that their tone is in moſt reſpeƈts far ſuperior to the Organs built at the preſent time), is this, that they are totally unfit for the performance of the muſic of the day, which in the humble opinion of the writer, is a ſtrong argument in their favour, and an additional reaſon for their being retained ; for the muſic of the day is certainly very far from eccleſiaſtical in its ſtyle, and therefore far more deſerves turning out than the fine Organs of Schmidt, Harris, and others.

The reaſon why theſe beautiful inſtruments are ſo often deſtroyed is, that the clergy and thoſe in authority, are perſuaded by their organiſts that the inſtruments in queſtion are not fit to play upon; by which they mean that it is impoſſible to ſhow off upon them in the most approved fashion, for they have neither pedals, swell, or any of those complicated contrivances with which these modern *Music Mills* (as Mr. Jebb most aptly calls them in his Lectures on the Choral Service) are crowded. Every lover of true Cathedral Music must have experienced how much these modern alterations and additions to the Organ, mar the effect of that most devotional manner of performing the Church Service. In the chanting of the Psalms, the attention is continually drawn from the voices by the perpetual changing of stops and clattering of composition pedals, for the modern Cathedral Organist scarcely ever accompanies six verses on the same stops, or even on the same row of keys, and keeps up a perpetual thun-

dering with the pedals throughout
the Pſalms, when perhaps the choir
he is accompanying, confiſts of ten
little boys, and ſix or at moſt eight
men, three or four of whom are
either diſabled by old age, or a long
continued habit of drunkenneſs.
Happily, however, our choirs are
now in a fair way for improvement,
and it is ſincerely to be hoped that in
the courſe of a few years, ſuch caſes
as thoſe juſt alluded to will ceaſe to
exiſt, though even now ſeveral very
glaring inſtances might be pointed
out. But with regard to Organs,
they ſeem to become more and more
overpowering every day. Where
will it end? At preſent, in many
Churches the choir might almoſt as
well be ſilent, for the whole ſervice
is thundered by the Organ, ſo that
the voices are only audible at inter-

vals, and thofe very wide ones too. Lately, many Organifts have ufed the chorus ftops but little during Cathedral fervice, with the intention of allowing the voices to be better heard; but they forget that three modern heavily voiced diapafons, coupled to a full fwell (the fwell is now nearly as large as the great Organ, and contains often a double diapafon), and accompanied with pedal pipes, on a very large fcale, are far more overpowering than the brilliant chorus of the ancient Organ, which commonly confifted of feven or eight ftops only, the effect of which as it pealed along the vaulted roofs of our awful Cathedrals was truly thrilling, heightening the effect of the voices without overpowering them. Alas! it is now feldom to be heard; for though fome few of the old Organs

remain, they are fo altered and enlarged, that in moft refpects they
nearly refemble the tone of the modern Organ. Sufficient has now
been faid of the mifchievous confe-
quences of thefe very large Organs
in Cathedrals, and it now remains
to be fhown how they injure the
effect of the ordinary parochial fervice. The remark made in relation
to the Cathedral Organ, that it
drowns the voices, can only apply
to a certain extent to the parifh
Church Organ, as the finging is in
general fo execrable as to juftify the
Organift's playing with fome force,
in order that he may in fome degree
hide the defects both of the fchool
children and congregation, who generally make a point of finging half
a note below pitch.

But in other refpects the intro-

duction of a *Mufic Mill* into a parifh
Church is even more dangerous than
in a Cathedral, as the Cathedral
Organift is generally a good mufician, and even if he is not, the con-
ftant performance of the folemn fervices and anthems of Tallis, Farrant,
Gibbons, Childe, &c. &c. muft give
him fome idea what Church mufic
ought to be; but in a Parifh Church
the Organift is often a felf-fufficient
inexperienced perfon, with probably
a good deal of execution on his inftrument, who can ufe the pedals perfectly, and knows how to manage
(as far as the fhifting of them about
is concerned) all the contrivances
with which the immenfe Organ may
be crowded; in fhort, he confiders
himfelf as a firft-rate performer, and
perfuades other people that he is fo
too, and on the ftrength of this he

inflicts upon the congregation long
voluntaries, interludes, &c. which
confist either of his own vulgar ima-
gination, or selections from the last
new opera. Under the present state
of things, it is hopeless to look for
proper Parish Church Music, as it
now appears entirely unconnected
with any part of the Liturgy, inas-
much as the Psalms and Hymns of
the Church are left to the Priest and
Clerk alone, and the Music is only
used for the metrical psalms and
hymns, which are introduced between services and before sermons,
and the grave Gregorian Chant is
never heard. But by the retention of
old Organs, or, where new ones are
introduced, by having only small ones
without much variety, there will not
be so much opportunity for display,
and the music will be far less disgust-

ing than is generally the cafe. From what has been faid, it appears that large Organs are in every way objectionable, as they offer a great temptation to a good mufician to produce great effects, and in his excitement, if accompanying voices, often to forget them altogether, and the confequence is, that an Anthem frequently ends with an Organ folo inftead of a full Chorus of voices. As for a bumptious country Organift, with one of thefe *Mills* at his command, he is in his glory, and his hearers in amazement.

After fo much has been faid in favour of old Organs, it is but fair to ftate, that there are beyond all doubt fome parts of modern Organs which far furpafs thofe built from the reign of Charles the Second to the end of the laft century. Such

are the bellows, with all their contrivances for keeping the wind steady;
and the manufacture of the reed
pipes, which were formerly coarse
toned and very disagreeable, as they
still continue to be in France and
Germany. Nothing can exceed the
beauty of their tone at present; even
during the last ten or twelve years
their improvement has been very
great. Hill, Grey, and Bishop, the
principal Organ builders of the present time, seem to have arrived at
the height of perfection in these re-
spects, and if these were the only additions they made to the old Organs
of Schmidt, Harris, and Schnetzler,
nothing could surpass them, and
their restoration of these venerable
instruments would be in every way
perfect. The effect of Pedals in
Fugue playing is truly magnificent;

but in Englifh Organs the pedals are very inferior to thofe in Germany, as they confift in this country of only one fet of pipes, either a very large open or ftop diapafon, and feem to require fome connecting link between the Organ and Pedals. In Germany, there is a chorus upon the pedals as well as upon the manual, which feems to have the defired effect. But as Fugue Playing is not the chief object in an Englifh Cathedral, and the confequence of pedals, and *Pedal pipes more efpecially*, having been fo mifchievous, it is much to be defired that they fhould be removed from Cathedral Organs, certainly from the one that accompanies the choir, for why fhould there not be two, as is commonly the cafe in France and Germany; and then the *Mufic Mill* even might have a fine effect, coming from a distant part of the Church, and used only on extraordinary occasions. In the manufacture of the wooden pipes, the modern Organ builders seem to be in every way at fault, and that part of an Organ appears now to be hurried over or totally neglected; if this is not the case they muft have loft the art of making them, and the sooner they avail themselves of the specimens which may still be seen of Schmidt's the better, since these cannot owe all their beauty and sweetness of tone to time, as is often supposed (though this may in some measure be the cause), for Schmidt is said to have been very careful in choosing the material he used, both that it should be without knots and also that it should be perfectly free from sap.

It is difficult to find out what kind of wood is ufed at prefent for wooden pipes, as it is now the fafhion to paint them all over with rud, perhaps with the intention of hiding their defects. The writer of thefe pages is acquainted with a cafe where the wooden pipes of a fmall barrel-organ, built for a Country Village Church by one of the firft rate Organ builders in London, all fplit open. The Rector of the Parifh fent to the eftablifhment where the Organ was built, and the perfon who came down to repair it actually nailed each pipe up. *What would Father Schmidt have thought of fuch a proceeding?*

It is now time to give fome account of the Organs built in England fince the Reftoration of King Charles the Second up to the prefent time, which the writer propofes to do in regular order, giving alſo ſome particulars as far as can be collected of the Organ builders, as well as their Organs, beginning with *Father Schmidt*.

CHAPTER I.

Uring the Rebellion all the Organs in England were deſtroyed by order of the Parliament, with all other Church furniture, which was conſidered as appertaining to the Romiſh ritual; ſo that at the Reſtoration, when Choral Service was about to be re-

vived, the difficulty of obtaining
Organs feems to have been very
great, for tradition fays, that at that
time there were only four Organ
builders in England, Dallans, Loofe-
moor of Exeter, Thamar of Peterborough, and Prefton of York; but
as it was impoffible for thefe four to
fupply all the Cathedrals, College
Chapels, and Parifh Churches in
England, as they all wanted new
Organs at the fame time, early in
the reign of King Charles the Second
premiums were offered to foreign
Organ builders to fettle in this country. Bernard Schmidt, a German,
was the firft to come over, and to
him we owe many of the fineft
Organs in the country. The vignette at the head of the chapter reprefents the Organ cafe generally
adopted by Schmidt, and is one from

which he feldom deviated in general arrangement. The Organ of St. Paul's Cathedral, which he built, was defigned by Sir Chriftopher Wren, to be in keeping with the Stalls, &c. and executed by Gibbons. It differs entirely from the example given, but it is the only exception of Schmidt's with which the writer is acquainted.

Dr. Burney gives fome account of Schmidt in his Hiftory of Mufic, from which perhaps it will be beft to make an extract.

" Bernard Schmidt, as the Germans write the name, brought over with him from Germany, of which country he was a native, two nephews, Gerard and Bernard, his affiftants; and to diftinguifh him from thefe, as well as to exprefs the reverence due to his abilities, which

placed him at the head of his pro-
feſſion, he was called *Father Schmidt*.
The firſt Organ he engaged to build
for this country was for the Royal
Chapel at Whitehall, which being
haſtily put together, did not quite
fulfil the expectations of thoſe who
were able to judge of its excellence.
It was probably from ſome ſuch
early failure, that this admirable
workman determined never to en-
gage to build an Organ upon ſhort
notice, nor for ſuch a price as would
oblige him to deliver it in a ſtate of
leſs perfection than he wiſhed. And
I have been aſſured by Snetzler, and
by the immediate deſcendants of thoſe
who have converſed with Father
Smith, and ſeen him work, that he
was ſo particularly careful in the
choice of his wood, as never to uſe
any that had the leaſt knot or flaw

in it; and so tender of his reputation, as never to waste his time in
trying to mend a bad pipe, either of
wood or metal, if it had any radical
defect; he instantly threw it away
and made another. This, in great
measure, accounts for the equality
and sweetness of his stops, as well
as the soundness of his pipes to this
day."

Schmidt's Organs were seldom
very large, and in general contained
from about fourteen to twenty stops,
and their compass was short, containing four octaves from C to C,
with the addition of A A and G G,
which additions are called short octaves, so that the Key-board appears
to extend from C to B, and the A
and G are so contrived, that the C♯
sounds A, and the B sounds G. His
Organs generally consisted of Great

and Choir Organ, and feldom contained many Solo Stops; but when
they were introduced, they were
placed in a feparate little Organ,
called *the Echo,* which confifted of
only two octaves from C in alt. to
middle C, and was placed over the
Keys below the other pipes, behind
the centre panel, which may be un-
derftood by referring to the woodcut
at the head of the chapter.

The following table will give fome
idea of the Stops contained in his
ordinary Organs:

GREAT ORGAN.

Open Diapafon	1	Twelfth . .	6
Stopt Diapafon	2	Tierce . . .	7
Flute * . .	3	Sefquialtra . .	8
Principal . .	4	Cornet . . .	9
Fifteenth . .	5	Trumpet .	10

* The Flute in Schmidt's great Organs is of
metal, and on a large fcale, and was called the
Block Flute.

CHOIR ORGAN.

Stopt Diapafon	11	Principal . .	13
Flute . . .	12	Fifteenth . .	14

ECHO.

Open Diapafon	15	Cornet . .	17
Principal . .	16	Trumpet . .	18

There are, however, very few remaining in their original ftate; the Echo has nearly difappeared and a Swell generally has been fubftituted for it: in the earlier Organs of Schmidt there were no Echos, and they muft have been far better without them, as they gave an opportunity to introduce very trifling mufic, fo that the writer, attached as he is to Schmidt's Organs, can fcarcely regret their removal. Schmidt had to contend with a very formidable rival in Harris, who arrived in this country from France, foon after Schmidt came from Germany.

* " About the latter end of King
Charles the Second's reign, the mafter of the Temple and the benchers,
being determined to have as complete an Organ erected in their
Church as poffible, received propo-
fals from both thefe eminent artifts,
backed by the recommendation of
fuch an equal number of powerful
friends and celebrated organifts, that
they were unable to determine among
themfelves which to employ. They
therefore told the candidates, if each
of them would erect an Organ in
different parts of the Church, they
would retain that which, in the
greateft number of excellencies fhould
be allowed to deferve the preference.
Smith and Harris agreeing to this

* See Dr. Burney's Hiftory of Mufic, page
437. Vol. IV.

propofal, in about eight or nine months each had, with the utmoſt exertion of his abilities, an inſtrument ready for trial. Dr. Tudway living at that time, the intimate acquaintance of both, ſays that Dr. Blow and Purcell, then in their prime, performed on Father Smith's Organ, on appointed days, and diſplayed its excellence; and, till the other was heard, every one believed that this muſt be choſen.

Harris employed Monſieur Lully, organiſt to Queen Catharine, a very eminent maſter, to touch his Organ, which brought it into favour; and thus they continued vying with each other for near a twelvemonth.

At length Harris challenged Father Smith to make additional reed-ſtops in a given time; theſe were the Vox-humana, Cromorne, the double Courtel, or double Baſſoon, and ſome others.

The ſtops, which were newly invented, or at leaſt new to Engliſh ears, gave great delight to the crowds who attended the trials; and the imitations were ſo exact and pleaſing on both ſides, that it was difficult to determine who had beſt ſucceeded. At length the deciſion was left to Lord Chief Juſtice Jefferies, afterwards King James the Second's pliant Chancellor, who was of that ſociety, and he terminated the controverſy in favour of Father Smith; ſo that Harris's Organ was taken away without loſs of reputation, having ſo long pleaſed and puzzled better judges than Jefferies.

The Honourable Roger North, who was in London at the time of the contention at the Temple Church, says in his Memoirs of Music, that the competition between Father Smith and Harris, the two beft art-ifts in Europe, was carried on with fuch violence by the friends of both fides, that they " were juft not ru-ined." Indeed, old Rofeingrave af-fured me, that the partifans for each candidate, in the fury of their zeal, proceeded to the moft mifchievous and unwarrantable acts of hoftilities ; and that in the night, preceding the laft trial of the reed-ftops, the friends of Harris cut the bellows of Smith's Organ in fuch a manner, that when the time came for playing upon it, no wind could be conveyed into the wind-cheft."

Harris built in general much larger Organs than Schmidt, and intro-duced many Solo ftops, both in the Echo and Choir Organs, fo that it is not improbable that Schmidt was obliged to introduce the Echo with its folo ftops into his Organs, in order that Harris might not get before him in public eftimation.

The Organ at Chrift Church, Oxford, was built by Schmidt when Doctor Aldrich was Dean, about the year 1680, and it had only a Great Organ and Choir Organ, and contained about the fame number of ftops as the example given without the Echo.

Doctor Aldrich was a great lover of Choral Service, and compofed feveral Services and Anthems in the beft choral ftyle, and would not have allowed any light Mufic to be performed at Chrift Church, which perhaps may account for the abfence of the Echo in the Chrift Church Organ; it was repaired about eighteen or twenty years ago by Mr. Bishop, and a small swell (from C to fiddle G), and common Pedals without separate pipes were added; it is now a very fine instrument, and quite sufficient to accompany the Choral Service, indeed far too powerful for the present wretched choir of Christ Church, which is a disgrace to the authorities.

The touch is the worst part about Schmidt's Organs, and is very disagreeable to those unaccustomed to play upon them, feeling as though cotton wool was placed under each key; but this surely might easily be altered. The bellows, in common with all Organs built anterior to the present century, supplied the windchest in a very irregular manner, and caused the Organ to sound tremulous; there were generally two sin-

gle bellows, as his Organs were feldom large enough to require more.

The great beauty of Schmidt's
Organs confifts in the fweetnefs and
brilliancy of the wooden pipes. Doctor Burney mentions an Organ, in
the poffeffion of the Honourable
Roger North, who died in 1733,
built by Father Schmidt, which,
though compofed entirely of wooden
pipes, was, as he faid, " fpritely and
infinitely more fweet than any one
of metal he had ever heard." The
Chorus is alfo very fine and very
brilliant in effect, though not quite
fo much fo as the Chorus afterwards
introduced by Snetzler in his Organs,
which though extremely brilliant, is
almoft too fhrill, and when heard in
a fmall building rings unpleafantly in
the ears. In Schmidt's Organs every
note tells, and the bafs is very firm,

and fpeaks decidedly; not one note
is ftronger than another throughout
the inftrument, which is a great advantage, and one not to be met with
in the modern Organs; for the bafs
in the new Organs overpowers the
treble and the middle parts.

Schmidt feems to have built a
great number of Organs from about
1680 to 1706; all his largeft inftruments were built during that period,
thofe of Durham Cathedral, the
Temple Church, St. Paul's, and Trinity College, Cambridge.

The Organ of the Temple Church
is generally confidered Schmidt's
mafterpiece, and though additions
have been made by Byfield, and lately
by Mr. Bifhop, it retains all the original pipes in great Organ and Choir
Organ. The fwell was conftructed
by Byfield, and perhaps ftill contains

the pipes of the original Echo. This Organ is remarkable for poffeffing quarter tones, fo that there is a difference of tone between G fharp and A flat, and alfo between D fharp and E flat. Originally, this arrangement occurred only in the Choir Organ and Great Organ, and it feems to have been introduced either as an object of curiofity, or to render it in fome way more perfect than *its rival*, fince probably Harris was unprepared for the novel contrivance.

This arrangement has fince been carried by Mr. Bifhop, in his late additions, throughout the fcale of the three fets of keys. The quarter tones are places above the fharps, which they refemble in appearance though not in fize, being only half the length of the others. By this arrangement of the key-board, it is poffible to play

in all the keys, major and minor, in
perfect tune, which is not the cafe
with common Organs, requiring
however a perfon well acquainted
with this peculiar key-board to avail
himfelf of its ufe. Mr. Bifhop alfo
added pedal pipes, new bellows, con-
cuffion valves, compofition pedals,
and all the modern inventions. The
reed ftops are very coarfe, as were
all Schmidt's, and to render the inftrument perfect they ought to be
replaced by new ones. This Organ
is at prefent a grand inftrument,
though far too large for the Temple
Church, even as it was five years
ago, and now of courfe infinitely
more fo.

The Organ of St. Paul's Cathedral is alfo a celebrated work of
Schmidt's, erected in 1694, and is
infinitely more effective than that of

the Temple Church, from being placed in a building more fuitable to its magnitude. The magnificent chorus of this Organ feems to be *duly appreciated* by the Organift, as the writer has often heard the greater part of the Choral Service of this Cathedral accompanied on the full Organ. The laft time he attended the fervice, it is but fair to ftate that this was not the cafe, and he therefore hopes that an improvement in the fyftem may be looked for, though the pedal pipes were as overpowering as ever. This Organ, as well as that of the Temple Church, retains much of the original work. The fwell was added by Cranz, foon after fwells were invented, and it has undergone two other repairs fince, the firft of which was by Meffrs. Orhman and Nutt early in the present century, and the second in 1826 by Mr. Bishop, who added the celebrated Pedal pipes, and renewed the Chorus stops. It was in this instrument that Mr. Bishop first introduced the Concussion Valves, now in such general use, and thus secured what had never been before achieved, the steadiness of the wind. At the same time the glass windows were removed from the fronts of the Organ. Dr. Burney in speaking of this Organ says, that it was reported that "notwithstanding the power and chorus of this admirable instrument, several more excellent stops were made for it, which lay many years useless in the vestry; but for which Sir Christopher Wren, tender of his architectural proportions, would never consent to let the case be sufficiently capacious to receive."

It is the opinion of Mr. Bifhop (who difcovered in the wind-cheft of this Organ another flide, for which there were no pipes), that it had been intended for a double Diapafon, with which ftop Schmidt, as a German, was probably acquainted, for in Germany thefe ftops were not uncommon in his time, and perhaps long before.* This conjecture feems highly probable, as there is no doubt that, to contain a double Diapafon in addition, the Organ cafe would neceffarily have to be much enlarged. Handel held this Organ in great ef-

---

* The German Organs have alfo keys for the feet, called Pedals, an invention of a German, named Bernhard, about the year 1400. Thefe command certain pipes, which to increafe the harmony, are tuned below the Diapafons.—Sir J. Hawkins' Hiftory of Mufic. Vol. IV. p. 150.

timation, and ufed frequently to play upon it.

The Organ in the Chapel of Trinity College, Cambridge, is another famous inftrument of Schmidt's. It was built in 1708, during the mafterfhip of the celebrated Doctor Bentley, of whofe club in London Father Smith was a member. The erection of this Organ, together with the repairs of the Chapel, which were carried on under the aufpices of the Mafter, in direct oppofition to the wifhes of the Fellows, gave rife, amongft other things, to the ferious quarrels which took place between Bentley and his College, and which nearly coft him his Mafterfhip. Schmidt died before the Inftrument was finifhed, as will be feen from the following quotation of a College document in Bifhop Monk's Life of

Bentley, p. 161. " He did not live to complete the Organ of Trinity; it was finifhed by tuning and voicing by his fon in law Xtopher Schrider, according to a refolution of the Maf-ter and Seniors, May 3, 1708." Sir John Hawkins feems doubtful as to the exact time of his death, but tells us " That the name of Smith occurs in the lifts of the Chapel eftablifh-ment from 1703 to 1709 inclufive, as Organ-maker to the Chapel, and alfo to Queen Anne. He had a daughter married to Chriftopher Schrider, a workman of his, who fucceeded him in his places." Since the firft erection of the Organ many additions and alterations have been made in it from time to time : By-field added a fwell ; Avory, a fmall fet of pedal pipes; and afterwards, Meffrs. Flight and Robfon, who were employed to repair and make alterations in it, injured it greatly by cutting the pipes, to render the pitch higher.*

In 1834 great additions were made; in fhort, the Organ was almoft re-built by Mr. Gray, and about three years fince, fome of the ftops were renewed by Mr. Hill, and a new Key-board was added. It now re-tains but little of Schmidt's work (at leaft in its original ftate), except in the Choir Organ. The Open Dia-pafons, though very powerful, have none of the fweetnefs of tone ufually fo remarkable in Schmidt's Organs. On the whole it is a fine inftrument,

---

* Schmidt's Organs were generally below concert pitch, and great numbers have been altered by cutting the pipes, though the confe-quences have not in all cafes been fo lamentable as in that of Trinity College.

though far inferior in fweetnefs and brilliancy of tone to the Organs of the Temple Church, St. Paul's, and others which remain more in the ftate in which Schmidt left them. The Reed Stops in this inftrument, by Mr. Gray, are extremely beautiful, efpecially the Cremona, which is exquifite.

The Organ of Durham Cathedral is a very fine one of Schmidt's, though not fo well known as thofe of St. Paul's, Trinity College, Cambridge, and the Temple Church. It feems from the original contract between the Dean and Chapter of Durham, and Father Smith, that this Organ was to have originally confifted of Great Organ and Choir Organ only, though an addition was made to it a few years after it was firft fet up, by Schmidt himfelf, and from the number of pipes introduced, it feems not improbable that this was an Echo. It has alfo undergone feveral repairs fince, firft by England, who renewed the Reed Stops and made extenfive repairs; and fecondly by Buckingham, who introduced a double Diapafon in the great Organ. Within the laft year it has been put into the hands of Mr. Bifhop, who has added pedal pipes, new chorus, &c. &c. The inftrument is now nearly twice the fize it was at firft; the two fronts being placed farther apart than in the original arrangement, to give room for the additions.

The writer cannot but think the additions lately made to this Organ unneceffary, as the inftrument was perfectly effective before; at the fame time he does not fear in this cafe the ufual confequences of increafing the fize of a Cathedral Organ, viz. the deftruction of the Choral Service, fince the management is in the hands of perhaps the firft Cathedral Organift in England, and one who thoroughly appreciates the folemn Choral Services. The writer cannot here refrain from expreffing his unbounded admiration of the celebration of the daily fervices of this Church, which reflects the greateft credit upon the authorities. The manner in which it is conducted is not only better but more reverent than in any other Cathedral Church in England, there being a full Choir at every Service, and the Mufic being almoft entirely of a grave and ecclefiaftical character. The writer could alfo point out inftances of the rubric being more ftrictly obeyed there than elfewhere; but he feels that in a book of this kind fuch remarks would be out of place.

But to return to the Organ. The writer, through the kindnefs of Mr. Henfhaw, the Organift of Durham Cathedral, has obtained a copy of the original agreement between the Dean and Chapter of Durham and Smith, relating to the erection of the prefent inftrument; and it is in every way fo unlike the prefent mode of carrying on fuch matters, that he inferts it here at full length, hoping that it may intereft fome of his readers who may be curious in fuch matters.

"A. D. 1683.

" Articles of agreement covenanted, concluded, and agreed upon the eighteenth day of Auguft in the five and thirtieth year of the reign of our

Sovereign Lord Charles the Second by the grace of God King of England, Scotland, France and Ireland, Defender of the faith. Between the Rt. Honble John Sudbury doctor of divinity, Dean and the Chapter of Durham of the Cathedral Church of Chrift and bleffed Mary the virgin of the one part and Bernard Smith of the city of London Organ maker of the other part as followeth.

" Imprimis. It is agreed by and between the s^d parties and the s^d Bernard Smith for himfelf, his Executors, and adminiftrators, doth hereby covenant, promife, and agree to and with the s^d Dean and Chapter and their fucceffors by thefe prefents that he the s^d Bernard Smith for and in confideration of the feverall fums of money hereinafter mentioned fhall and will before the firft day of May

which will be in the year of our
Lord one thousand fix hundred and
eighty five at his own proper cost and
charges make and fitt up in the Organ loft of the sᵈ Cathedral Church
of Durham a good, perfect, laudable,
and harmonious great Organ and
Choir Organ with a Cafe of good
found and fubftantiall Oak wood according to a draught or modell of
an organ in parchment whereon or
whereunto all the sᵈ partys have fub-
fcribed their names at or before the
time of fealing and delivering of thefe
prefents.

" Item it is agreed by and between
the sᵈ partys that the sᵈ Bernard Smith
fhall make in the sᵈ great organ thefe
feventeen ftops. viz. Two open diapafons of Mettall containing one hundred and eight pipes. A ftop diapafon
of wood containing fifty four pipes. A

principall of Mettall containing fifty four pipes. A cornet of Mittall containing nynety fix pipes. A quinta of Mittall containing fifty four pipes. A fuper Octave of Mittall containing fifty four pipes. A Holfluit of wood containing fifty four pipes. A block flute of Mittall containing fifty four pipes. A fmall Quint of Mittall containing fifty four pipes. A mixture of three ranks of pipes of Mittall containing one hundred and fixty two pipes. A trumpett of Mittall containing fifty four pipes. And in the Choir organ five ftops, viz, A principal of Mittall in the front containing fifty four pipes. A ftop diapafon of wood containing fifty four pipes. A voice Humand of Mittall containing fifty four pipes. A holfluit of wood containing fifty four pipes. And a fuper octave of Mittall containing fifty four pipes.

"Item it is agreed by and between thefe parties that the s^d great Organ fhall have a back front towards the body or weft end of the Church which fhall be in all things and re-fpects like to the fore front both in pipes and carving. And all the pipes belonging to the two diapafon ftops fhall fpeak at will in the s^d back front as in the fore.

"Item in confideration of which work by the s^d Bernard Smith to be done and formed in the manner and form aforefaid the s^d Dean & Chapter for themfelves and their fuccef-fors do covenant and grant to and with the s^d Bernard Smith his Ex-ecutors and adminiftrators by thefe prefents in manner and form follow-ing that is to fay that the s^d Dean and Chapter fhall and will well and

truly pay or caufe to be pay^d unto
the s^d Bernard Smith his Executors
Adminiftrators or affigns the fum of
feven hundred pounds of good and
lawful money of England at three
feveral payments that is to fay Two
hundred thirty three pounds fix fhillings and eightpence thereof in hand
at or before the fealing and delivering
hereof the receipt whereof the s^d
Bernard Smith doth hereby acknowledge and confefs and thereof and of
every part & parcel thereof doth
clearly acquit exonerate & difcharge
the s^d Dean and Chapter

by thefe prefents other two hundred
thirty three pounds fix fhillings and
eightpence thereof when the s^d whole
organ or organs is or are brought
into the s^d Cathedral Church and
ready for fitting up and other two
hundred thirty three pounds fix fhil-

lings and eightpence being the refidue thereof and in full amount of
the faid fum of feven hundred pounds
when the whole Organ is fitt up
and in every refpect finifhed according to the true intent and meaning
of thefe articles. And further that
the faid Bernard Smith fhall have
and take to his own ufe benefit and
charge the old Organ now belonging
to the faid Cathedral Church and all
the Materialls thereunto belonging
Provided the s^d Bernard Smith fhall
not or do not remove take nor carry
away the s^d old Organ till the new
organ be ready for fitting up as aforefaid.

"And laftly whereas the pipes of the
two fronts of the s^d great Organ and
the front pipes of the s^d Choir Organ
are to be painted and guilt according
to the beft way & mode of painting

& guilding of Organs at the proper coſt & charges of the sᵈ Bernard Smith. It is hereby agreed by and between the sᵈ parties that if the sᵈ Bernard Smith do well and ſufficiently perform all the aforeſaid works in making finiſhing and ſitting up the sᵈ new organ to the ample ſatisfaction and content of the sᵈ Dean and Chapter That the ſaid Dean and Chapter ſhall pay or cauſe to be payᵈ unto the ſaid Bernard Smith his Exʳˢ admʳˢ or aſſigns the ſum of fifty pounds of good and lawfull money of England and in full ſatisfaction for the painting and guilding the sᵈ organ.

" In witneſs whereof to the one part of theſe articles remaining with the sᵈ Bernard Smith the sᵈ Dean and Chapter have put this Chapter ſeal, and to the other part remaining with the sᵈ Dean and Chapter the sᵈ Ber-

nard Smith hath put his hand & feal
the day & year above written.

" Signed fealed and delivered in
the prefence of

WILLIAM WILSON.

Jo. SIMPSON."

Receipt of Father Schmidt on
receiving fifty pounds of the Dean
and Chapter of Durham for additional ftops in the year 1691.

"Received of John Rowell Twenty
four pounds being the laft payment
and in full of Fifty Pounds given to
me by the Worfh[1]. The Dean and

Chapter of Durham for work done
at ẙ Organ

      I ſay recᵈ

        By me

Ber: Smith

    In the Collegiate Church of South-
well, Nottinghamſhire, is an Organ
built either by Schmidt or his nephews, a ſmall inſtrument, but of
remarkably ſweet tone. It conſiſted
only of Choir Organ and Great Organ, and the compaſs ſeems to have
been from either C or D to GG in
full compaſs, without ſhort Octaves,
which was ſeldom the caſe in Smith's
inſtruments. Snetzler added a ſmall
ſwell and renewed ſome of the Chorus Stops, and England afterwards

added a Trumpet in the Great Organ, and a Dulciana in the Choir Organ. This Organ is remarkable for poffeffing the fweet toned wooden pipes of Schmidt, and brilliant chorus of Snetzler. The Choir Organ is placed in front, in a feparate cafe, as is ufual in England, where choral fervice is performed.

Perhaps it may not now be uninterefting to give a lift of fome of the Organs built by Schmidt and his nephews. Thofe which now are deftroyed, or removed from their original pofitions, are diftinguifhed by a ftar.

St. Paul's Cathedral, erected a. d. 1694.

The Temple Church, 1687.

*The Royal Chapel, Whitehall.

*The Royal Chapel of St. George, Windfor.

*St. Margaret's, Weftminfter,†
    1676.
St. Clement's Danes.
St. Peter's, Cornhill.
St. Mary, at Hill.
St. Mary, Woolnoth.
St. James's, Garlick Hill.
*Eton College Chapel.

† The old Organ by Father Smith in St. Margaret's, Weftminfter, was built in 1676, as the following quotation from Sir John Hawkins' Hiftory of Mufic, will fhow: " Of thefe children (the children of the celebrated Henry Purcell) we have only been able to trace one, viz. a fon, named Edward, who was bred up to mufic ; and in July 1726, was elected Organift of St. Margaret's, Weftminfter. Upon infpection of the Parifh Books, for the purpofe of afcertaining this fact, it appears the Organ of this Church was built by Father Smith in 1676, and that he himfelf was firft Organift there, and played for a falary."

Father Smith, it appears, alfo repaired the old Organ of Weftminfter Abbey, in 1694, from a note in the fame hiftory, page 508, vol.

Theatre, Oxford.†
Chrift Church, Oxford.
St. Mary's, (Univerfity Church),
    Oxford.
Trinity College Chapel, Cam-
    bridge, 1708.
St. Mary's, (Univerfity Church),
    Cambridge, 1697.

---

iv. " Farther, that he (Henry Purcell) is a
fubfcribing witnefs to an agreement, dated 20th
of July, 1694, between the Dean and Chapter
of Weftminfter, and Father Smith for repairing
the Abbey Organ." This muft be the fmall
Organ, reprefented in the print of the Choir of
Weftminfter Abbey, at the Coronation of King
James the Second, in Sandford's Book of the
Coronation. It was placed under one of the
arches on the north fide of the Choir, and had
a fmall projecting Organ loft over the Stalls.

† That at the Theatre was taken down, and
removed to the Church of St. Peter in the eaft
at Oxford, and a new one, made by Byfield and
Green, erected in its ftead. Sir John Hawkins'
Hiftory of Mufic. Vol. iv. p. 355.

*Winchefter Cathedral.

Durham Cathedral, 1684.

Southwell Collegiate Church, Notts.

High Church, Hull.

All Saints, Derby.

Hampton Court Palace Chapel.

The writer has in his poffeffion two Chamber Organs of Schmidt's; they refemble his Church Organs much in tone and in all other re-fpects, both having been originally below concert pitch, and both have had the misfortune of having their pipes cut, to render the pitch higher; but they feem not to have fuffered much, as they are ftill very fweet toned. The larger one contains fix ftops, and has two fets of keys and two wind chefts; but the upper row of keys acts upon both wind

chefts, fo as to form the Great Organ. The Stops are: Stopt Diapafon,
wood; Open Diapafon, wood; Open
Flute, wood; Stopt Flute, metal;
Fifteenth, metal; Furniture, metal.
The vignette at the end of the chapter reprefents the fmaller one.

CHAPTER II.

CCORDING to Dr. Bur-
ney, " Smith had not been
many months here before
Harris arrived from France, with his
ſon René or Renatus, an ingenious
and active young man, to whom he
had confided all the ſecrets of his

art. However they met with but little encouragement at firſt, as Dallans and Smith had the chief buſineſs of the kingdom; but upon the deceaſe of Dallans, who died while he was building an Organ for the old Church at Greenwich, 1672, and of the elder Harris, who did not long ſurvive him, the younger became a very formidable rival to Smith."

The etching at the head of this Chapter, repreſents one of Harris's Organ caſes: but he does not ſeem to have been conſtant, like Smith, to any one particular form, ſo that his Organs are not ſo eaſily recogniſed at firſt ſight as thoſe of his rival. The Organ caſes of St. Sepulchre's, London, and St. Nicholas, Newcaſtle upon Tyne, reſemble the example given, and they were built before the death of the elder Harris.

But the inftruments of this builder
may be readily afcertained by examining the mouths of the front pipes,
which are not funk, as is ufually the
cafe, but are raifed above the furface
of the pipe, fo that the mouth is more
prominent than any other part of it.
The Organs made by this workman
and his fon, are certainly only fecond
in excellence to thofe of Schmidt.
His Diapafons are both fweet and
rich, and his chorus is vivacious and
ringing, even more fo than Schmidt's,
and his reed ftops, though far inferior to thofe made at prefent, are
alfo fuperior to his.

In many refpects there is a refem-
blance between the Organs of thefe
two workmen; but though Harris's
wooden pipes are excellent, they
never poffefs that peculiar reedy and
brilliant tone which is fo charming

in all Schmidt's.   Harris feemed to have been as ambitious of excelling in the manufacture of metal pipes as Schmidt was in thofe of wood, often ufing that material for his Stop Diapafons.

No lifts of the ftops contained in the Organs mentioned in this work have been given, as the writer has found them fo nearly identical in all the different inftruments of the fame maker, that he thinks it is only neceffary to give a lift of thofe which each builder ufually introduced. Harris's Organs generally contained from about twenty-two to thirty ftops, diftributed throughout the three fets of keys, in a manner of which fome idea will be gained by the following table :

Great Organ.

1. Open Diapafon.
2. Ditto.
3. Stopt Diapafon, fometimes metal.
4. Principal.
5. Twelfth.
6. Fifteenth.
7. Tierce.
8. Mounted Cornet, five Ranks.
9. Sefquialtra.
10. Furniture or Mixture.
11. Larigot.
12. Trumpet.
13. Clarion.

Choir Organ.

1. Open Diapafon.
2. Stopt Diapafon.
3. Flute.
4. Principal.
5. Fifteenth.
6. Cromorne.
7. Baffoon.
8. Vox Humane.

Echo.

1. Open Diapafon.
2. Stopt Diapafon.
3. Principal.
4. Cornet.
5. Fifteenth.
6. Trumpet.
7. Cromorne.

Harris's moſt celebrated Organs are thoſe of St. Sepulchre's, London, which however is now much changed ſince its firſt erection in 1667, and Doncaſter, Yorkſhire.

The writer is inclined to believe that the invention of the fwell, though generally afcribed to Green, was the invention of the younger Harris. During the laft Summer he fpent a few days in examining as many of the older Organs of the City Churches as he could get accefs to. He was much ftruck with the grandeur of the tone of the Organ of St. Dioni- fius, commonly called St. Diony's, fituated in a very remote part of the city. From the tone, and general appearance of the inftrument, he is inclined to afcribe it to the younger Harris, though he was told by the Organift that it was one of Father Schmidt's.* This inftrument pof- feffes a fwell, which has the appear-

---

* All old Organs in this country are called Father Schmidt's by thofe unacquainted with Schmidt's peculiarities.

ance of being a part of the original Organ; indeed the whole inftrument feems to be in the ftate in which it was originally left. Its compafs is from D to GG full compafs, and the fwell goes down to fiddle G, whereas the ufual echo of Harris and Schmidt only extended to middle C. The Choir Organ, as well as the Great Organ, contains an open Diapafon. The reed ftops are very good for the time in which they were made, and are very numerous; for inftance, there is a Cromorne in both the Choir Organ and Swell, and a Baffoon and Voxhumane in the Choir Organ. This inftrument is fupplied with wind by four pairs of bellows. The writer now gives a lift of the Organs of Harris with which he is acquainted, upon the fame plan as the lift of Schmidt's.

St. Sepulchre's, London,†A.D.1667.

St. Andrew's, Holborn, do. erected there 1699.

St. Mary's at Axe, London.

St. Lawrence, Jewry, do.

St. Brides, do.

St. Nicholas's, Newcastle upon Tyne, (about) 1670.

Doncaster, Yorkshire, 1738.

*Ely Cathedral, Cambs.

*Jesus College Chapel, Cambridge.

Winchester College Chapel, rebuilt by Green.

Wolverhampton Coll. Church.

Bristol Cathedral, 1685.‡

---

† The writer supposes many other Organs in the Churches of the City of London to have been built by Harris, but he does not insert them in the list, as he has no authority for the supposition beyond his own opinion.

‡ In the years 1681 and 1685 in the Deaneries of Towgood and Levett, £300. or more

The Organs of Wolverhampton and St. Andrew's, Holborn, feem to have been conftructed from the fpoils of the famous one built by Harris for the Temple Church; for Dr. Burney fays, " Harris's Organ, after its rejection at the Temple, was part of it erected at St. Andrew's, Holborn, and part in the Cathedral of Chrift Church, Dublin; but about thirty years ago, Byfield having been fent for to repair the latter, he prevailed on the Chapter to have a new inftrument, taking the old Organ in

was laid out in mending the floor and beautifying the Church, painting the eaft end of the Choir and other works, and in making a fine timber cafe for the new Organ, erected by the contribution of the Dean and Chapter and many other well difpofed perfons, at the expence of £550. in the whole to Mr. Renatus Harris, Organ builder. Barrett's Hiftory of Briftol, p. 290.

exchange as part of the payment. Soon after, having had an application from the Corporation of Lynn Regis in Norfolk, to build them a new Organ for St. Margaret's Church, he wifhed very much to perfuade them to purchafe the inftrument made by Harris, which had been a fecond time excommunicated; but being already in poffeffion of an old Organ, they determined to have a new one; and by the advice of the author of this book," (Dr. Burney) " employed Snetzler to conftruct one, which he did, very much to his own credit, and their fatisfaction, confifting of thirty Stops, three ranks of Keys, and full compafs.

" That part of the Organ for the Temple Church by Harris, and fent to Dublin, was fold after the death of the elder Byfield, to Wolverhampton for £500. It ftill ftands in the Church of that town, and is thought a very good inftrument."

The Organ of St. Andrew's, Holborn, feems not to have been paid for fo foon as it ought to have been, from the following note, page 539, vol. iv. of Sir John Hawkins' Hiftory of Mufic. " Dr. Sacheverell, having been prefented to the living of St. Andrew's, Holborn, found an Organ in the Church, of Harris's building, which having never been paid for, had from its erection in 1699 been fhut up. The Doctor, upon his coming to the living, by a collection from his parifhioners, raifed money enough to pay for it."

Sir John Hawkins alfo tells us that Harris in the latter part of his life retired to Briftol, in which neighbourhood he built feveral Organs.

CHAPTER III.

Schreider. Schwarbrook,
&c.

CHREIDER, a German, was a workman in Schmidt's Organ building eftablifhment, and about the year 1710 fucceeded him in his appointment as Organ builder to the Royal Chapels. He feems to have built very much in the fame ftyle as his mafter. His Organs are not numerous; but fuch as remain fpeak very well for his fame. The Organ of Weftminfter

Abbey, which is a very fine inftrument, is his work. This is fo well known, and fo defervedly appreciated, that it is needlefs to make any remarks upon it. This Organ gains much of courfe from the nature of the place in which it is heard, and from the mafterly manner in which it is touched by the prefent Organift, Mr. Turle, whofe accompaniment of the Choral Service is quite a model for that kind of Organ playing. Schrieder alfo built the Organ of St. Martin's in the Fields. This laft Organ was the prefent of King George the Firft, as the following note from Dr. Burney fhows. " Schreider, who built the Organ of St. Martin's in the Fields, which King George the Firft prefented to the Church, upon being chofen Churchwarden of the parifh, foon after his Majefty's arrival in England." This Organ has given place to another built by Gray.

Schwarbrook, who was alfo a German, was a workman in the eftablifhment of the elder Harris, who, according to Dr. Burney, "built feveral Organs but repaired more." The Organ of St. Saviour's, Southwark, was originally built by Schwarbrook, but in all probability little of his work remains.

Byfield, *Bridge* and *Jordan* came after Schreider and Schwarbrook. Byfield feems to have held a high place in public opinion; and his Reed ftops are ftill in good eftimation. He was in all probability in the eftablifhment of the younger Harris, and was married to his daughter. He afterwards took into partnerſhip Bridge and Jordan, who had each ſeverally ſhown themſelves excellent workmen. Jordan built the Organ for the Chapel of the Duke of Chandos, at the time that Handel was domeſticated with the Duke, and regulated the muſical ſervice of his Chapel.

Theſe builders ſeem generally to have introduced the Swell in their Organs. Many of the Organs in the city of London and its neigh-bourhood are built either by one or other of theſe artiſts, or all in con-junction. In ſhort they had the whole buſineſs of the country, until the arrival of Snetzler. There was alſo a builder in London about that time of the name of *Cranz*, who ſeems not to have been thought much of, and to have built but few Organs.

He added the Swell to the Organ of St. Paul's Cathedral, and built one or two for fome of the City Churches.

CHAPTER IV.

NETZLER feems to have arrived in England fome-where about the year 1735. He owed his fame chiefly to the Organ he built for Lynn Regis in Norfolk, being recommended to the Corporation of that town by Dr.

Burney. In this Organ was a double Diapafon, which then muft have been a novelty in this country, he alfo firft introduced his Dulciana Stop which ever fince has continued popular, and has been employed in almoft every Organ fince built. His inftruments are remarkable for the purity of their tone, and the extreme brilliancy of their Chorus Stops, which in this refpect furpaffed any thing that had been heard before in this country, and which have never fince been equalled. His reed ftops were alfo much better than thofe built before his time. His Organs though they are more brilliant than their prede-ceffors, fall fhort of that fulnefs of tone which characterized thofe of Schmidt, Harris, Schreider, &c. &c. but they are neverthelefs moft charm-ing inftruments.

He had but an imperfect pronunciation of the English language, which gave him a very quaint way of expressing himself. There are two stories well known of his strange manner of giving vent to his feelings. One was on the occasion of his new Organ at Halifax in Yorkshire being first tried; Dr. Wainwright, Organist of Manchester, being sent for to open it, annoyed Snetzler by playing very rapid passages upon his Organ, and he exclaimed, "He do run over de keys like one cat, and do not give my pipes time to speak." He also told the Churchwardens of Lynn, upon their asking him what their old Organ would be worth if repaired, " If they would lay out a hundred pounds upon it, perhaps it would be worth fifty." He made very beautiful Chamber Organs, and usually introduced a hautboy stop upon another wind chest in a small swell box, the action of which he attached to the ordinary action, thus saving the expense of another set of keys. These instruments generally had glass doors in front of the pipes, and the cases were made of mahogany, and had much the appearance of an old-fashioned bookcase. He also sometimes made very small Organs in the shape of a set of drawers, with a writing desk at the top, which being opened, discovered the keys and stops. These instruments usually contained four stops, and the pipes were very curiously packed in a small space. His compass was generally from E in alt to GG, but with short octaves, though in some of his grander instruments he carried the compass down to GG without short octaves, as it is done at the prefent time. His Organs are ftill very numerous; there are feveral in different parts of Yorkfhire. The writer now gives a lift of the ftops generally employed by Snetzler in his larger Organs.

GREAT ORGAN.

1. Open Diapafon.
2. Stopt Diapafon.
3. Principal.
4. Fifteenth.
5. Twelfth.
6. Sefqualtra, 4 ranks.
7. Cornet, 5 ranks.
8. Trumpet.
9. Clarion.

CHOIR ORGAN.

1. Stopt Diapafon.
2. Dulciana to Fiddle G or Tenor C.
3. Flute.
4. Principal.
5. Fifteenth.
6. Hautboy, a fancy ftop.

SWELL FROM E TO FIDDLE G.

1. Open Diapafon.
2. Stopt Diapafon.
3. Principal.
4. Fifteenth.
5. Cornet.
6. Trumpet.
7. Hautboy.
8. Clarion.

The keys of Snetzler's Organs were

longer than they had been before, and the sharps and flats very narrow, (like the new Piano Forte keys,) and had a piece of ivory or bone on the top of the sharps, only the sides being black as the naturals.

List of Organs built by Snetzler.

Lynn Regis, Norfolk.
St. Mary's, Nottingham.
One at Huntingdon, if not two.
Halifax, Yorkshire.
Rotherham, Yorkshire.
Whitehaven, Cumberland.
St. Peter's College, Cambridge.
German Lutheran Church, London.
St. John's, Hackney, near London.

His Chamber Organs are very numerous.

Snetzler lived to a very great age, and died either at the end of the laft, or the beginning of the prefent century. He is faid to have faved fufficient money to return and fettle in his native country, which he accordingly did; but having been fo long accuftomed to London porter and Englifh fare, he found in his old age that he could not do without it, fo he came back to London, where he died.

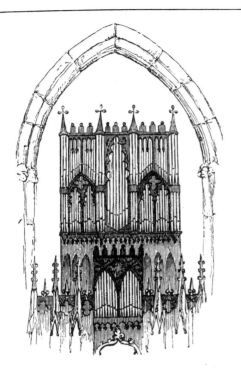

CHAPTER V.

REEN was a contemporary of Snetzler, and towards the end of the laſt century ſeems rather to have taken the lead of him. In all probability he was brought up

in the eftablifhment of Byfield, Bridge
and Jordan, as in the earlier part
of his career as an Organ builder
he was in partnerfhip with Byfield.
He was very much patronifed by
King George the Third, for whom
he built feveral Organs. The Organ
of St. George's Chapel, Windfor,
built by Green, was prefented to the
Chapel by the King, and was erected
about the year 1780. He alfo built
the Organ of Salifbury Cathedral,
which was a prefent to the Cathedral from that King. The occafion
of this prefent being made was as
follows; the King, happening to
pafs through Salifbury, at the time
the Cathedral was under repair, en-
quired of the authorities how the
works were going on, and being told
by them that their funds were falling
very fhort, and that amongft other

things, they were afraid they fhould
not be able to bear the expenfe of a
new Organ, which was very much
wanted, their old one being worn
out; the King defired the Dean and
Chapter to accept a new Organ from
himfelf, as a Berkfhire Gentleman,
the King's favourite refidence, Windfor Caftle, being in that county.

Green alfo built a fmall Organ for
the King's private ufe, which has
lately been repaired with fome additions, by Gray, for His Royal High-
nefs Prince Albert.

The writer is obliged to confefs
that he cannot join in the general
admiration of Green's Organ building. He certainly carried his fyftem
of voicing the pipes to the higheft
degree of delicacy; but what he
gained in that way he loft in the
general effect of the inftrument. In

his Diapafons, though the quality of tone is fweet, at the fame time, it is very thin, and his Chorus is entirely deftitute of either fulnefs or brilliancy of tone. His Choir Organs are pretty toned, and would make nice chamber Organs, but they want firmnefs. One would fuppofe that Green was anxious in his inftruments to emulate the tone of a mufical fnuff box, rather than that of an Organ.

His compafs and general arrangement of the ftops is much the fame as Snetzler's, though he fometimes carried that of his largeft Organs down to F F F, as in the Windfor Organ. He was the firft to adopt the white naturals and black fharps in the Key-board of large Organs, in the fame manner as in the Pianoforte, though Snetzler had fometimes done the fame in the Key-boards of Chamber Organs.

Green, under the patronage of the King, became quite the head of his trade, and was employed in all parts of the kingdom. His Chamber Organs are very nice inftruments, (in fhort all his Organs are Chamber Organs on a large fcale,) his great Organs having much the fame effect as any other enclofed in a general fwell, which really was the cafe in the Windfor one, before it was repaired by Gray. He unfortunately brought in a ftyle of Organ building which had many imitators, and from which the trade is only juft recovering.* Avory and England both copied in a great meafure his peculiar

---

* It is evident from the late productions of Mr. Hill, that he is now fully alive to the faults

voicing of the pipes, though their Organs are certainly a great improvement upon his.

The following is a lift of fome of the many Organs built by Green.

St. George's, Windfor.

Private Organ, Windfor Caftle.

Salifbury Cathedral.

alluded to in the Organs of Green and his fucceffors.

The Organ of St. John's College, Cambridge, is one of the fineft modern inftruments with which the writer is acquainted. The Diapafons are remarkably good, and the Chorus has almoft arrived at the ancient brilliant tone fo much praifed in thefe pages. The new Organ at Worcefter is alfo very fine, and almoft more brilliant than that of St. John's College; in both thefe inftruments, and more efpecially in that at Worcefter, the Choir Organs are harfh and unpleafant, which is much to be regretted, as in other refpects they are fuperior to any built fince the early part of the laft century.

Canterbury Cathedral.

Rochefter Cathedral.

New College Chapel, Oxford.

St. Katharine's Hofpital, London.

St. Botolph's Aldgate, London.

Sleaford Church, Lincolnfhire.

Lichfield Cathedral.

CHAPTER VI.

Avory. England. &c.

VORY who was a fhocking drunken character, and a perfon not in any way to be depended upon, being generally drunk and often in prifon for debt, was neverthelefs an excellent workman, when he was once fet to work. He imitated Green a good deal, but was much his fuperior. In his time pedals and even pedal pipes were coming into ufe in England, and are generally to be found in his larger Organs. In 1804 he

built the fine Organ of King's College Chapel, Cambridge, which is
one of his beft inftruments. The
Diapafons are rich and fonorous, and
the Chorus is very brilliant. The
Choir Organ is very fweet and deli-
cate in its tone, but at the fame time
not fo miferably thin as thofe of
Green. He alfo added pedals (what
are now called toe pedals) and fmall
pedal pipes to the Organs at Trinity College Chapel and St. Mary's
Church in the Univerfity of Cambridge. The laft Organ he built
was for the Cathedral Church of
Carlifle, in 1808. He died during
the time that this Organ was being
put up. This was a very nice though
fmall Organ when the writer played
upon it fome few years ago; but
fince that time it has been altered
and enlarged by Mr. Hill. In quality

of tone it much refembled the Organ in King's College Chapel, Cambridge, though a much fmaller inftrument.

The following Organs were built by Avory.

Winchefter Cathedral.
Carlifle Cathedral.
King's College Chapel, Cambridge.
St. Margaret's, Weftminfter.
Croydon Church, Surrey.
St. Stephen's, Colman Street, London.

England was the next Organ builder of importance. His Organs are very fine, and very much refemble Avory's. His eftablifhment did not continue for many years, and an attempt was made to carry on the bufinefs by his fon-in-law, Nichols; but it did not fucceed. His Diapafons are very fine, and his Chorus brilliant.

He built the following Organs.

Newark Church, Nottinghamfhire.
St. Stephen's, Walbrook, London.
St. Margaret's, Lothbury, London.
St. Martin's, Lincoln.
Organ in the Chorifter's School, Lincoln.

About the fame time were feveral other Organ builders of more or lefs importance; *Lincoln*, *Ruffel*, and others. *Flight* and *Robfon* built many Organs in the beginning of the prefent century.

Elliott was alfo doing a great deal of bufinefs; he built the Organ removed a few years back from the Royal Chapel at St. James's; and the

Organ of the Royal Chapel at Whitehall he fitted into Schmidt's old cafe.
Thefe three laft mentioned eftablifh-
ments were the fchool of the prefent
race of Organ builders. *Hill*, *Gray*,
and *Bifhop*.

*Lift of fome of the more important Or-
gans by Hill, Gray, and Bifhop.*

Hill.

Town Hall, Birmingham.
York Cathedral.
Worcefter Cathedral.
Ely Cathedral.
St. Peter's, Cornhill, London, &c.
Royal Chapel, St. James's Palace.

Gray.

Eton College Chapel.
Melton, Leicefterfhire.
Kennington.

St. Martin's in the Fields.
Chefter Cathedral.

Bifhop.

St. James's, Bermondfey.
St. Giles's, Camberwell.
St. Edmund, the King and Martyr,
Lombard Street.
St. Michael's, Coventry.
St. Mary's, Aldermanbury.
St. Mary's, Abchurch.

At the time the paffage in p. 61,
refpecting the invention of the Swell
by Harris went to prefs, the writer
had not feen the following paffage
quoted in the Chronicles of London
Bridge. "The 'Spectator' of February
the 8th, 1712, thus fpeaks : 'Whereas
Mr. Abraham Jordan, fenior and
junior, have, with their own hands,
joynery excepted, made and erected,

a very large Organ in St. Magnus'
Church, at the foot of London
Bridge, confisting of four sets of
keys, one of which is adapted to the
art of emitting sounds by swelling
the notes, which never was in any
organ before; this instrument will
be publicly opened on Sunday next,
the performance by Mr. John Ro-
binson.—The above-said Abraham
Jordan, gives notice to all masters
and performers, that he will attend
every day next week at the said
Church, to accommodate all those
gentlemen who shall have a curi-
osity to hear it.'" Chronicles of
London Bridge, page 457. This
instrument still exists, but has been
much altered and modernised by Par-
sons, at present only three of the
original four sets of keys remain.

The question is now left to the

reader's judgment. The author takes alſo this opportunity of adding the following liſt of inſtruments which ſhould have been inſerted after the biographical notice of Byfield, Bridge and Jordan.

Liſt of Organs by Jordan, Bridge and Byfield.

Jordan.

Duke of Chandos's Chapel, Cannons.

St. Magnus the Martyr, London Bridge.

Bridge.

Chriſt Church, Spitalfields.

St. Leonard's, Shoreditch.

St. Anne's, Limehouſe,

Yarmouth, Norfolk.

Byfield.

St. Mary's, Rotherhithe.

Grantham, Lincolnſhire.
St. Mary R. Briſtol.*
St. John's College, Oxon.
The Theatre, Oxon.
Organ in Magdalen College Hall.

* The entrance into the Church is at the great weſt door, to which you aſcend by ſteps ; the door is eight feet in breadth and twelve high, within which is built a great ſtone gallery, on which is a grand magnificent Organ, being in all fifty-three feet high from the ground to the top of the crown pannel ; the great caſe is about twenty feet ſquare, contains one great and leſſer Organ. The muſical part was executed by Meſſrs. Harris and Byfield, and the whole coſt 846*l*. 7*s*. Barrett's Hiſtory of Briſtol, p. 574.

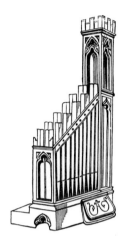

CHAPTER VII.

HE laſt chapter of this book will be entirely devoted to Organ Caſes, which for the laſt century and more have been ſo taſtelefs in their deſign, as to become an eye-ſore in every Church in which they have been placed. The Caſes which were built by Schmidt, in the

latter part of the feventeenth century,
are far better than any thing that has
been built fince, for although the
detail is not ecclefiaftical, ftill the
old form is kept up, and the general
appearance is the fame as thofe erected
in Germany and Flanders, from the
latter end of the fourteenth to the
end of the fixteenth century, and the
carved work is bold, and confifts only
of open work panelling in imitation
of foliage and flowers, with large
angel's heads, and at the prefent time
with the affiftance of a hundred and
fixty years, they really look very venerable, efpecially when they have
diapered pipes, which is the cafe in
the Durham Cathedral Organ, and
fome others. The writer of thefe
pages would recommend that thefe
old Cafes fhould be allowed to remain
for two reafons; firft, becaufe they

furnish an example of the right form of Case being preserved in an age of bad taste; and, secondly, becaufe nothing half fo good can be procured at prefent.

The Cafes of Harris are much more elaborate than thofe of Schmidt, and many of the details are thofe which were in common ufe in fitting up the apartments of the court and nobility of France, during the reign of Louis the Fourteenth; wreaths of flowers and indelicate fat cupids, by way of angels, with drapery ufed for every purpofe in the world but to cover their nakednefs. It is needlefs to comment further on fuch ornaments, as it muft be evident to every one that, to fay the leaft of them, they are very much out of place in a Church, and offenfive to the feelings of right-minded perfons.

After the time of Schmidt and Harris, Organ Cafes became plainer and meaner every year, and the old form was entirely deferted. Snetzler, Green and others, in the middle of the laft century, enclofed their Organs in Cafes as much like a fquare box as poffible, the fide being quite as broad as the front, and the trypticlike form, which was kept up by Schmidt by making the front overhang on each fide, was difcontinued.

Early in the reign of George the Third attempts were made to reftore the Gothic ftyle, at leaft in the reftorations made in old Churches; with what fuccefs may be feen by examining the Stalls at Weftminfter Abbey, the Altar and Organ Screens at St. George's Chapel, at Windfor, and other works executed about the fame period. Green, who was at that

time at the height of his popularity,
and was very much patronifed by
King George the Third ; was obliged
to conform to the prevailing tafte,
and began to engraft innumerable
pinnacles and incorrect Gothic details upon his taftelefs boxes, and their
effect was, if poffible, worfe than the
plain ones which preceded them.
Many of our Cathedrals, College
Chapels, and Parifh Churches, are
disfigured by thefe unfightly Organ
Cafes, which become every day larger
and more heavy looking, and the
ornamental parts refemble the barley
fugar ornaments we fee about Chrift-
mas time in paftry cooks' windows,
difplayed in all their glory on a
twelfth cake. From time to time
flight improvements were made in
the details, though they were inju-
dicioufly applied. Every part of a

Church has been copied for the Organ Cafe, and attempts have been made at one time, to make the Organ look like a tomb, at another like a fcreen, at another the canopies of the ftalls have been placed on the top of the Organ, and latterly, as if in defpair of producing any thing decent, the Organ has been put out of fight altogether.

In France, Belgium and Germany, there are many Organs ftill in exiftence which, with fome of the details correóted, would furnifh very good models for new ones; the details having (through frequent repairs in times of bad tafte) often been removed and replaced by ornaments in the ftyle of Louis Quatorze; but they remain in fuch a ftate, that with a little care and attention, and of courfe fome knowledge of Church

Architecture, a proper ecclesiastical Case might easily be made from them.

The writer now proposes to give some examples of this kind of Organ Cases, which have been kindly furnished by Mr. Pugin.

The two first are examples of a Cathedral Organ, which is a very rich design, and suitable only for a magnificent building, and, in addition to its being made of oak, and elaborately carved, is richly painted and gilded, and will therefore necessarily be very costly. It is intended to be placed at the side either of the nave or choir, and so constructed that the entrance to the Organ Loft is from the Triforium Gallery. It stands upon a richly carved bracket, and has a Choir Organ in front, and the pipes of the great Organ are placed in a Case in front of one of the

Clereſtory windows, of which it ought only to conceal a portion, and ſhould projeᏟt only three or four feet at moſt, which will be found ſufficiently large to contain all the ſtops neceſſary for the accompaniment of the Choral Service; the bellows ſhould be placed behind the Organ in the Triforium Gallery.

In the interior view of Lincoln Minſter, in Dugdale's Monaſticon, the Organ is ſo placed on the north ſide of the choir, the general effeᏟt of which is very good, though the Organ Caſe itſelf is in bad taſte, and almoſt deſtitute of ornament of any kind. This arrangement is very common on the Continent, and fine examples may be ſeen at Fribourg in Germany, Straſbourg, and Chartres in France, and many other places; thoſe mentioned retain much of their

original detail, and painting and gilding.

An Organ in a proper Ecclefiaftical Cafe has a very good appearance over the weftern entrance of a
Cathedral, but, in that cafe, there
muft alfo be a fmall Organ to accompany the fervice, on the north
fide of the Choir, above the ftalls,
under one of the arches of the Choir.
At the Cathedral of Amiens the
Organ is placed over the weft door,
and has its Cafe much in its original
ftate (though fome additions in the
Italian ftyle have been made to it,)
and retains the original painting and
gilding: it ftands upon beams ftretch-
ed acrofs the whole width of the
nave, under which is a groined roof
of oak painted blue, with the ribs
red and gold, and the vaulting blue,
powdered with golden ftars. The

Organ itfelf is for the moft part
blue, and the pipes are left their
natural colour.

It is to be hoped, now that the
attention of the public has been
drawn to the effect of decorative
colouring in Gothic buildings, that
it will in time be applied to every
part of a Cathedral and large Church,
and that Organ Cafes among other
things will not be paffed over. Any
perfon who has feen an ancient Organ, with all its proper decorations,
cannot but be difgufted with the ab-
furd attempts that have been lately
made in this country to produce a
Gothic Organ Cafe.

What can have a more diftreffing
effect than the cumbrous Organ at
York, with its details taken from the
Stalls, and its *iron* looking pipes?

Any large Organ placed over the

screen of a Cathedral muft deftroy
both the effect of the fervice, if the
congregation be affembled in the
nave, (as they undoubtedly ought to
be,) and alfo mar the fair proportions of the edifice ; and no where is
this improper arrangement more felt
than at York. Some of our Cathedrals offer a very good fituation for
an Organ where the Choir is carried under the centre tower, by plac-
ing it under the north arch of the
tower, where it now ftands at Winchefter, and might with great pro-
priety be placed at Norwich, Chi-
chefter, and feveral others. The
cuftom of diapering the pipes was
univerfal in our Englifh Cathedrals
before the great Rebellion, and for a
fhort time after the Reftoration the
cuftom was continued. The Organs
of Durham Cathedral, Chrift's Col-

lege, Cambridge, and the eaſt front of St. Mary's, Oxford, are ſtill diapered, as were alſo the old Organs of King's College, Cambridge, and New College, Oxford, the laſt of which was built by Dallaus about the year 1665.

The third example is ſuitable for the weſt end of a large Church, and therefore is not ſo elaborate as the one juſt given. The pipes being left the natural colour (which is frequently ſeen on the Continent) have a much better appearance than the immenſe maſs of gilding on our Organ pipes, which forms a curious contraſt to the meanneſs of the Caſes. The fourth deſign is intended for a village Church, and is very ſimple, and might be made of deal, but coloured as repreſented in the drawing. Such an Organ containing ſix Stops;

Stopt and Open Diapafon, Principal,
Fifteenth, Twelfth, and Sefqualtra,
with fhort compafs from C to C;
ought to be furnifhed by the firft
Organ builders for a hundred pounds.

The writer would recommend that
the Principal fhould be made of
wood as in Schmidt's Chamber Organs, which with the Diapafons
would form a good Choir Organ, as
he is well aware from long experience that a Village Choir will never
fing in tune with the Diapafons alone,
and the wooden Principal has the
effect of fomething between the Principal and Flute, (in fact Schmidt
called it an Open Flute,) and is not fo
fhrill as the Metal Principal. The
front Pipes will of courfe be Speaking
Pipes, as they are left without either
painting or gilding. The laft example is for a fmall Chamber Organ,

and may, at pleafure, be either more
or lefs ornamented. Like the larger
Organs it has doors or fhutters to
clofe over the pipes, which will be
found very ufeful in keeping out the
duft; the appearance when open
will be very much that of a triptyc,
as the infide of the doors is painted.
It is needlefs to add that fuch an
Organ Cafe is only fuitable for a
houfe built in the Gothic ftyle, or
an oratory, for which it feems more
efpecially adapted.